Listening to the Jewish Jesus

How a first-century rabbi still speaks to us today

Paul Luckraft

malcolm down

PUBLISHING

British Library Cataloguing in Publication Data
A catalogue record for this book is available from the British Library.

ISBN: 978-1-915046-65-9

Cover design by Esther Kotecha
Art direction by Sarah Grace

Printed and bound by CPI Group (UK) Ltd, Croydon, CR0 4YY

Endorsements

An excellent teacher on this subject, Paul tackles one of the most important and enriching themes of today as many seek to dig deeper into the Jewish roots of their faith, so long lost to the Gentile church.

Charles Gardner, Author and Journalist

Paul's focus on Hebraic thinking and his opening up of Hebrew idioms are vital to a correct understanding of the scriptures. By listening to the Jewish Jesus his life and teaching comes alive in a fresh way.

Dr Greg Stevenson, Co-leader of the Cranfield Hebraic Study Group and of Yqabetz, a Biblical and Hebraic Teaching Ministry

Paul enables us to hear Jesus' words as his contemporaries would have heard them. Many a mystery is solved and many a misunderstanding laid bare. Knowing these things will inform and enrich my own preaching.

Derek Bownds, Bible Teacher

Paul's book gives invaluable insight into the culture and customs at the time when Jesus walked on earth. It has made familiar scriptures burst into life with new meaning, revelation and understanding. I couldn't stop reading.

Mari McLoughlin, Church Leader

Part Two: Sermons and Stories

Part Three: Clues and Hints

Part Four: Other Puzzling Passages

Acknowledgements

This book is based upon years of study and hu[...] hours of sharing this material in various sma[...] and other larger settings. I am most grateful to t[...] teachers and writers who have guided me along [...] path of understanding. When compiling the [...] lessons, I drew extensively from several source[...] Suggested Reading in the back of this book car[...] acknowledge a few of these, but it is hoped the li[...] also encourage readers to pursue this topic further[...] pioneering research and expertise of those who devel[...] such studies on the Jewish Jesus has been inspiratio[...] but any errors in this book are entirely due to my o[...] misunderstandings.

It has been a privilege to pass on what I have gleaned fro[...] others on this subject. It has also been among the mos[...] enjoyable aspects of my own teaching and one that ha[...] been particularly appreciated by others. Those I taught often asked me where they could read more about this for themselves. Although many have already written on this subject (the Suggested Reading list could be a lot longer) such interest and hunger to know more encouraged me to collect these lessons together into a book, not only for them but for anyone starting out on this journey of discovery into the Jewishness of our master teacher.

original format of this material was therefore that notes to aid interactive teaching. Turning these into apters of a book was not a straightforward task, so I cided to produce a series of short talks first and then use ese to put together the final written version. I felt more mfortable with this method as it was one I was familiar ith from writing my first book, *The Wall and the Word* Iso published by Malcolm Down Publishing). If at times is obvious that what you are reading had this origin and ourney towards what you are holding now, then I hope it helps rather than hinders.

I am extremely grateful to all at my own church who gave me regular encouragement and support. Your feedback was invaluable. Thanks also to those who gave me opportunities to teach this material in various gatherings, either online or in person. Special thanks go to those who attended my sessions at the Foundations Bible School.

I am greatly indebted to Frances for her initial help in preparing the original manuscript and compiling the index, and also for managing my website. Do check this out, www.orchardseeds.com, where you will find the talks that accompany this book, and much more.

I am grateful to all at Malcolm Down Publishing for guiding me through the process of producing this book. Special thanks go to my editor, Louise, for her usual prompt and efficient work, and to Malcolm Down for his clear advice and expertise. Thanks also to the graphic designers for the front cover and to Clifford Hill for providing the foreword.

Foreword

Listening to the Jewish Jesus will be high up on the list of essential reading for serious students of biblical hermeneutics, but its unique value lies in its readability for non-scholarly Christians who want to know more about the life and teaching of Jesus.

Paul Luckraft, with his years of experience of classroom teaching of students, has an exceptional ability for presenting a scholarly script in an easily readable and interesting narrative. This book is packed with fascinating insights into the ministry of Jesus that lie hidden behind the writing of our English translations of the four gospels in the New Testament.

Each of the four sections in this book adds significantly to our knowledge and understanding of the teaching of Jesus as they are examined from an Hebraic perspective. My wife and I have listened to Paul on a number of occasions when he has been teaching on the idioms used by Jesus that are not clearly presented in our English translations. We have both been fascinated by the facts that Paul has uncovered, and we have each benefited greatly from his teaching.

In his Introduction, Paul says, 'Jesus used many Hebraic idioms and colloquialisms. An idiom is an expression in common use in one language that makes no sense in a different language if translated literally.' I can personally endorse this. I was speaking to a meeting of ministers of the Lutheran churches in Germany and I referred to the need for unity in our pastoral work in London. I said, humorously, that if we did not hang together, we would hang separately. The interpreter told the astonished assembly that in London if the clergy did not unite, they face the death penalty!

I learned a lesson that day that I've not forgotten. It makes me grateful to Paul Luckraft for the huge amount of work that he has put into this book, which illuminates so much of the teaching of Jesus that is lost in our English translations. He uses little things that we can so easily miss because we do not read from the same perspective as the crowds and individuals would have heard when he first spoke them. The Jewishness of Jesus was part of the culture shared by his disciples and by the ordinary people who listened to him on many occasions, such as when he fed the five thousand or sat in the boat speaking to the people on the beach. That same culture was the perspective from which the gospel writers presented the word of the Lord.

I particularly loved the teaching on discipleship that this book illustrates in the relationship between Rabbi and disciple. It is highlighted here in a way that I had not perceived in the action of Peter getting out of the boat and walking towards Jesus.

There are many more stories like this that are highlighted in this book that will be memorable for every reader – both the scholarly and the ordinary reader. I warmly commend *Listening to the Jewish Jesus* to all those who are seeking a closer walk with Jesus.

The Revd Dr Clifford Hill, MA, BD, PhD

Introduction

He Opened His Mouth and Spoke

The record of Scripture clearly shows that from birth to death Jesus lived as a Jewish man among Jews. This aspect of our Lord's identity is now generally accepted in the field of biblical studies, and is becoming more widely recognised within the main streams of Christianity. Those who acknowledge his Jewishness find themselves understanding and appreciating Jesus in fresh and deeper ways.

Personally I have found my own Bible study and teaching to be greatly enhanced through this. In particular, I have discovered that the illumination provided by the Jewishness of Jesus shines through most clearly on those occasions when 'he opened his mouth and spoke'.

This expression sounds strange to us, with its seemingly unnecessary overuse of verbs. This is because it is an example of a Hebraism, a phrase that is particularly Hebraic in nature. In fact, it is a slightly shortened version of 'and he opened his mouth, and taught them, saying' which occurs just before Jesus delivers what we call the Sermon on the Mount (see Matt. 5:2).

Modern translations tend to tidy this up. For instance, we might simply have 'he began to teach them'. But the clumsiness of the expression, with its threefold use of a verb, exists in the Greek where it should not naturally occur any more than we would expect it to in English. However, in Hebrew verbs tend to dominate and a phrase like this makes good sense to a Hebrew reader, and listener, as a way of emphasising the significance of what follows. It is not that at times Jesus opened his mouth (goldfish-like!) without uttering any words, or that he occasionally spoke (mumbled!) without opening his mouth. Rather, this phrase signals that here is something of prime importance that should be listened to carefully.

To illustrate this further, consider a similar phrase: 'he lifted up his eyes and saw'. This expression is found in a story that Jesus told about a rich man and a beggar called Lazarus. Both die and go their separate ways, one to Hades and the other to Abraham's bosom. At one point the rich man 'looked up and saw' Abraham with Lazarus by his side (Luke 16:23).

Again the doubling of the verb indicates the Hebraic nature of Jesus' storytelling. Not surprisingly, we find this phrase in the Old Testament. In Genesis 24:63, the Hebrew reads that Isaac, while meditating in the fields one evening, 'lifted up his eyes, and saw, and behold . . .' What he saw must have delighted him. Camels! But not just camels – his bride-to-be, Rebekah, was arriving! The following verse then records that Rebekah also 'lifted up her eyes and saw' Isaac.

As before, modern translations tidy this up a bit, so we might have 'he (or she) looked up and saw', but the repeated verbs, superfluous to us, stress the Hebraic nature of the phrase as well as the importance of the occasion.

We need not assume that both were looking down at their feet just beforehand. Rather, here is a key moment in the life of Isaac and in the whole Genesis account. Love at first sight, perhaps!

This sort of Hebraic phraseology occurring in the gospels has led to the suggestion that at least some of the gospel material was originally written down in Hebrew, maybe even a whole gospel, most likely that of Matthew. Scholars debate this idea but consensus remains elusive as no such manuscripts have been found, and so the matter remains a complex and contentious one, outside the scope of this book. Nevertheless, even without external evidence of this kind, there is plenty of internal verification in the gospel texts that Jesus spoke as a Jew to Jews. His verbal expressions and methods of teaching provide the most convincing evidence of his Jewishness. This is what we will explore in this book.

So what can we expect to find? What will we hear as we listen to the Jewish Jesus?

Firstly, Jesus used many Hebraic idioms or colloquialisms. An idiom is an expression in common use in one language that makes no sense in a different language if translated literally. It has its own special meaning which someone outside the culture or who is not a native speaker will find difficult to understand.

For instance, in English the phrase 'it's raining cats and dogs' would cause much scratching of heads if put word for word into another language. What is happening to our pets? Similarly, the phrase 'eat your heart out' could cause great consternation!

We need a better grasp of the Hebraisms within the gospels if we are to fully understand what Jesus is saying to us. Otherwise, as western readers we may not always catch what he means.

Secondly, Jesus often referred to his own scriptures, which we call the Old Testament. Sometimes these references are clear to us, but at other times they are more obscure. He dropped hints, provided clues and made allusions which Jewish listeners would readily pick up, but which non-Jewish listeners can miss, especially if we don't read the Old Testament regularly, or commit it to memory as Jews of the time did. This means we often fail to see things that are significant in the words of Jesus. Help is needed!

Then, finally, in listening to the Jewish Jesus we will encounter aspects of first-century Judaism with which we are unlikely to be familiar. It was a religious world with its own culture, very different from ours in many ways. As modern western readers, we will have to come to terms with this if we are to understand the context in which Jesus ministered and spoke.

In the chapters that follow, we won't be covering every word of Jesus. That is neither possible nor necessary. After all, not everything Jesus said is mysterious or cryptic. We will focus on the main passages where an explanation of some kind is helpful.

While this book may not be totally comprehensive, we will cover a lot of ground. Some chapters are based upon a single passage, or occasionally just one verse. Others will take you on a tour of several parts of scripture. Clearly the gospels will feature a great deal but so will portions of the Old Testament. Be prepared to work through each chapter with an open Bible, and an open mind, ready to think through what you are learning. Consider this book as a companion to your Bible reading. It may be that some of the points made here are already familiar to you from elsewhere. If so, then may this book be to you like a storeroom where you find new treasures as well as old (see Matt. 13:52).

One aim of this book is to help those who teach the Bible. If that is you, then I hope you will regard this as a resource to equip you to explain the scriptures more accurately. This may mean correcting previous misconceptions, but we are all still learning. If you are not a Bible teacher, then do consider giving this book to someone who is. Even those writers and teachers who acknowledge that Jesus was Jewish still find it difficult at times to interpret what he said.

The gospels were written in Greek but Jesus was Jewish. If these Greek texts faithfully preserve the teachings of Jesus then evidence of his Jewishness should be there somehow – and it most definitely is, even if rather hidden at times. Uncovering this evidence is a delightful experience, full of 'light bulb' moments.

If Jesus 'opened his mouth and spoke' as a Jewish teacher, then that is how we should listen to him. These pages offer a fresh hearing for Jesus, especially for those who believe in him but are bewildered at times by what he said. For all of us who claim to follow Jesus we need to hear him better.

May you be greatly blessed as you listen afresh to the Jewish Jesus.

PART ONE

A Rabbi and His Disciples

Chapter One

Like Father, Like Son

Matthew 4:18-22

Come, follow me

Our main purpose in this book is to examine some of the specific teachings of Jesus, but before we do so there are two features of first-century Judaism that require our attention, namely 'rabbi' and 'disciple', and in particular what they meant to each other. The rabbi-disciple relationship is a dominant feature of the gospels, and a clear understanding of this is essential for a proper reading of the gospel text, especially when it comes to the words of Jesus, whether spoken to his chosen Twelve or to others.

Jesus was addressed as 'rabbi' on many occasions (some say up to forty times) and by many different kinds of people, not just his own disciples. But what did it mean?

In Jesus' day the term 'rabbi' was commonly used to describe teachers of the Jewish Law, but it was not yet an official title. Only after the fall of Jerusalem and the destruction of the Temple in AD 70 when Judaism had to redefine itself, did the title 'rabbi' acquire a new significance. A ceremony then took place involving the

23

laying on of hands (*semikhah*) as someone was set apart to lead and teach others.

But in the time when Jesus was teaching, there were no formal qualifications for becoming a rabbi. Rather, it was a courtesy title for someone who was accepted as a teacher and respected as such by others. As an example closer to home, in my earlier career as a schoolteacher I was regularly addressed as 'sir'. But this by no means indicated I had received a knighthood or was entitled to the capitalised version, 'Sir'! It was merely a respectful way of acknowledging the teacher-pupil relationship.

The word 'rabbi' is derived from the Hebrew *rav*, which simply means 'great'. To call someone 'rabbi' therefore conveys the sense of 'my great one' or 'my master'. This does not have to refer specifically to someone who teaches you. It can be anyone you look up to. But it was mostly applied to teachers of Torah and its meaning could be summed up as 'my master teacher of great learning'.

Jesus was regularly esteemed in this manner by those who heard him. He clearly gained a reputation as a rabbi as large crowds gathered to listen to him, in some cases travelling long distances and staying all day. Not everyone may have wanted to bestow such honour on him, but those who did would readily echo the words of another highly regarded Jewish teacher of the day, Nicodemus: 'Rabbi, we know you are a teacher who has come from God' (John 3:2). That was the only recognition that truly mattered.

It was also expected that a rabbi at that time would have followers, known as disciples, even if only a handful. Behind this well-known word, 'disciple' (Hebrew, *talmid*;

Greek, *mathetes*), lies a whole world which is far from readily appreciated. The relationship between a rabbi and his disciple was much closer than that which we would normally associate with a teacher and his student. It was more like that of a father and son.

Disciples weren't just expected to listen to a rabbi and learn from what he said. They were also to observe him in everything he did and then do the same, even when he was temporarily absent or no longer with them. A rabbi was regarded as an example to be followed, someone to be imitated in conduct and character. That placed a huge responsibility on the rabbi who had to live out his own teaching so his disciples could see it in action. He showed them how to live life in every way. They were to learn how to think like him and how to 'walk his walk'. In effect, his disciples were undergoing intensive training as his apprentices so that one day they would be like him.

Certain passages in the New Testament illustrate this well. For instance, in the upper room just before the meal we call the 'Last Supper', Jesus washes the feet of his disciples. He then comments: 'You call me "Teacher" and "Lord", and rightly so, for that is what I am. Now that I, your Lord and Teacher, have washed your feet, you also should wash one another's feet. I have set you an example that you should do as I have done for you' (John 13:13-15).

In his first letter to the Corinthians, Paul instructs the new believers: 'I became your father through the gospel. Therefore I urge you to imitate me' (1 Cor. 4:15-16), later adding, 'Follow my example, as I follow the example of Christ' (1 Cor. 11:1).

Paul is telling them that because he imitates Jesus in every way, effectively following him as his rabbi, Paul's converts can safely imitate him in turn, as this will make them disciples of Jesus too. We will pick up this point again in the next chapter.

Paul also calls himself their 'father', illustrating the father-son aspect of discipleship, something which is also seen in the way he refers to Timothy as 'my son' (1 Tim. 1:2, 18, 2 Tim. 1:2, 2:1). For instance, Paul's reference to Timothy as 'my true son in the faith' (1 Tim. 1:2) is commonly regarded as indicating that Paul led Timothy to faith in Christ, perhaps during Paul's first visit to Lystra, and that as a result Timothy looked to Paul to provide him with the initial teaching and discipleship that he required. We shall see later how strong the rabbi-disciple relationship was compared to family ties. For now, we can sum it up as 'like father, like son'.

This relationship also meant that the rabbi was fully responsible for his disciples. If they did anything wrong then he was to blame! Any actions of theirs that drew the disapproval of others would reflect badly on their rabbi. We see this in the gospels when the Pharisees challenged Jesus about his disciples (Mark 2:18, 2:23-24, Matt. 15:2). Why weren't they fasting like other disciples did? Why were they eating the corn in the field on the Sabbath which was unlawful? Why were they breaking the tradition of the elders and not washing their hands before eating? Such disgraceful behaviour implied that Jesus was not training them properly!

We can see now that the standard call of 'Follow me', which Jesus issued to those he chose to be his disciples, meant more than just joining him in some classes or getting a bit of extra education. It was a life-changing moment, involving total commitment which would last for years. They had left everything behind, including families and businesses, to start anew with their rabbi. At one point Peter declared, 'We have left all we had to follow you' (Luke 18:28). Jesus reassured him that, ultimately, he wouldn't lose out. 'No-one who has left home or wife or brothers or sisters or parents or children for the sake of the kingdom of God will fail to receive many times as much in this age, and in the age to come eternal life' (Luke 18:29-30).

From this it is clear how costly discipleship could be. By accepting the call to follow his rabbi, a disciple indicated he was open to change and would accept the challenge to walk in his master's footsteps. A disciple also had to be willing to endure whatever hardship was necessary for his learning experience, as well as to agree to become part of a close-knit group with a common life and purpose. The only way to acquire the right training and become like your rabbi was in the company of others on the same journey. This was the sort of relationship Jesus had with his disciples. In first-century Judaism, this mentoring concept was both self-evident and extremely effective.

Did many choose to become disciples? If you had done well in the usual stages of Jewish schooling, you might desire to go further and seek out a rabbi. The rabbi may agree to accept you, in which case he would say, 'Come, follow me.' But if at any time you weren't following properly, you would be told to go back to your father's house and take up his trade instead. Apparently, this happened quite frequently to would-be disciples at that time. We might wonder if this was the case with the four young fishermen Jesus called at the outset of his ministry: Simon Peter, Andrew, James and John (Matt. 4:18-22). Had they already tried to become disciples of another rabbi but been turned down and forced to return to fishing? We'll never know, but it's an intriguing thought. Perhaps Jesus saw something in them that others didn't and gave them a second chance.

A lot was expected of a disciple. Firstly, he had to memorise his teacher's words and be able to repeat them to others. Oral transmission was the main method then, so memorising the rabbi's teaching verbatim was essential, as was understanding his teaching methods and how he drew meaning from the scriptures.

In addition, a disciple had to learn his rabbi's traditions and methods of interpretation. Every detail was important: how he washed his hands, how he fasted, prayed, recited the blessings, and so on. A disciple was to imitate his rabbi in every way, not just in religious matters. The rabbi's home life and family relationships were also models to be copied. To reflect your rabbi in every way was now your first priority. If your rabbi did it, so did you.

We see this in action in the powerful drama of Peter walking on the water (Matt. 14:22-33). In this story we usually focus on Peter's initial courage or his later failing, but in doing so we can miss an important point. Why did he even try this in the first place? He was in a boat at night in the middle of Lake Galilee during a storm. What could possibly entice him to get out of the boat and go for a stroll? The answer is that he saw his rabbi, Jesus, walking on the water, so he wanted to do the same.

This is first-century Jewish discipleship at work. You want to be like your rabbi in every way. If your rabbi does it, you do it. What is more, you know you *can* do it, otherwise your rabbi would not have called you in the first place. Moreover, it would not have occurred to Peter to try walking on the water unless he had seen Jesus doing this first. His words, 'Lord, if it's you, tell me to come to you on the water' (Matt. 14:28) were a natural response to what he saw.

If a rabbi chose you as one of his disciples he was effectively saying, 'You have the potential to become like me.' This was a great honour, and so you applied yourself thoroughly to his words and his ways. You had faith in his judgement and his decision to call you to this life of following him. Of course, in the case of Peter getting out of the boat, it was still 'little faith', but it was a start. The other disciples never even tried, whereas Peter was already reaching out for a new level of discipleship.

We may read a mild rebuke in Jesus' question, 'Why did you doubt?' (Matt. 14:31), but let us also hear him saying, 'You have everything you need to do what I call you to do. I would never have called you if I didn't know you could do it.'

This incident is a good example of how Jesus taught as a rabbi. Here was a visual lesson, based upon personal experience not just spoken words. Everything about a rabbi's life was intended to be instructive for those following him. We saw earlier how by washing his disciples' feet, Jesus was providing an example to be followed. Wherever he went and whatever he chose to do had a deliberate purpose about it, to teach his disciples something. This also applied to his miracles and healings. Sometimes Jesus healed purely out of compassion but so often his major miracles came with a lesson attached. Look for this as you read these stories. Imagine you are there with him, as one of his disciples. Ask yourself, what would you have seen or felt as well as heard? What else was going on around him? What or whom was he looking at, for instance? Was he pointing to something perhaps? Use your imagination, not as an onlooker but as a disciple, someone wanting to imitate him in every way.

In this chapter we have begun to see how the relationship between Jesus and his disciples was typical of the time. But there were also two major differences, and we turn to these in our next chapter.

Chapter Two

By Whose Authority?

Matthew 21:23

In our previous chapter we looked at what it meant to be a rabbi and a disciple in the time of Jesus, and in particular at the significance of the rabbi-disciple relationship. We also began to see that Jesus' teaching style was rooted in Jewish tradition, and we will come across more examples of this during the course of our studies. But there were also some differences, one of which was over the matter of authority, which is the subject of this chapter.

Those who heard Jesus speak were in no doubt that he did so with authority, though their reactions varied considerably. The crowds were often amazed by it, even astonished: 'No-one ever spoke like this before! It's so unlike our usual teachers of the Law!' (Matt. 7:28-29, Mark 1:22, Luke 4:32, 36).

But for the religious leaders this was more worrying. For them, certain questions arose which needed clear answers: 'By what authority are you saying these things?' they asked. 'And who gave you the authority to do this?' (Matt. 21:23, Mark 11:28, Luke 20:2). These questions are very revealing and show how important authority was to them.

So where did Jesus get his authority from? And what did it mean?

We have seen that before AD 70 there was no formal office of rabbi, just teachers who carried the title informally out of popular respect. However, there was a convention in place to prevent anyone teaching whatever they wanted. You were constrained by what had come before. You were expected to teach in the name of your rabbi and those who had taught him. Thus, most religious teaching of the day was based on the tradition of quoting other rabbis. Typically you quoted Rabbi X, following Rabbi Y, following Rabbi Z, who said . . .

This may seem very stale and second-hand, but it showed you had learnt your stuff from others and were passing on their collective wisdom rather than merely giving your own opinion. Here was your chain of authority, your credentials, which would have been recognised by those who heard you. But, in certain cases, you were allowed to teach something new if you had received special authority to do so. This came about if two other already 'authorised' teachers publicly pronounced that you too had authority.

This explains the questions of the chief priests and elders mentioned above (Matt. 21:23). They needed to know who had authorised Jesus. This was about keeping control. Perhaps they also wanted to know if anyone else was behind his messages. Were others teaching these same things?

When Jesus was challenged in this way, he deftly turned the tables on his accusers by replying with another question about authority. What about John the Baptist's authority?

Where did he get his from? God or men? Now the religious leaders were stuck. They knew John didn't get his authority from their system and they couldn't claim he did without upsetting people who believed he was a true prophet. And if they said it came from God then they would stand accused of not believing and following his teaching. They had no answer, except the lame, 'We don't know', which allowed Jesus to sidestep the issue and force them to drop the whole matter (Matt. 21:24-27).

However, when it comes to Jesus' authority we have a much better answer than 'we don't know'. Jesus *had* received authority and in the highest possible way, from God the Father himself. It could be argued that Jesus had been authorised in the accepted way by two persons when at his baptism the Spirit descended on him and the Father spoke from heaven, declaring him to be his beloved Son with whom he was well pleased (Matt. 3:16-17). Later this was reinforced at Jesus' transfiguration when again the voice from heaven spoke, this time adding 'Listen to him!' (Matt. 17:5).

As mentioned in the last chapter, Nicodemus had no doubt about where Jesus' authority came from. 'Rabbi, we know you are a teacher who has come from God. For no-one could perform the miraculous signs you are doing if God were not with him' (John 3:2). Jesus also backed this up with statements of his own when he talked about being 'sent' and that 'my words are not just my own' (see, for example, John 7:28, 14:10, 24, also 17:2).

We now understand why the crowds were amazed at the end of the so-called Sermon on the Mount and commented on his authority (Matt. 7:28-29). Jesus had not quoted other rabbis! Indeed, his repeated response to 'You have heard that it has been said' was 'But I tell you' (see Matt. 5:21-22, 27-28, 33-34, 38-39, 43-44).

To speak in this way was to break the rules of authorised teaching. The phrase 'But I tell you' may not have been totally unique to Jesus, but its use aroused attention, even suspicion. Here Jesus was operating like someone who had an authority all his own. No-one had passed on to him what he was telling them. Hence his listeners were astonished. 'Can he *really* say that? Does he have authority?'

Jesus sits to teach

In our quest to listen to the Jewish Jesus more carefully, we will return to these three chapters of Matthew in due course. There are plenty of examples of Jesus teaching in a Jewish rabbinic manner in the Sermon on the Mount for us to unpack, though a full commentary on these chapters is beyond the scope of this book.

For now, we will simply note how Matthew introduces this section of his gospel: 'He went up on a mountainside and sat down' (Matt. 5:1). Matthew has Jesus seated before he 'opened his mouth and taught them, saying'. In Jewish culture, rabbis sat to teach, unlike in ours where a speaker or preacher usually stands. Of course, in reality on this occasion Jesus may well have been moving about as he taught, as is often portrayed in films at this point. Moreover, it is unlikely that Jesus delivered all this material on just one occasion. It was too important for that. More likely is that Matthew parcelled it all together for the purposes of his gospel. It is our western tradition of preaching or delivering sermons that designates Matthew chapters 5 to 7 as a 'sermon' rather than this being an accurate description of what happened at the time.

Nevertheless, Matthew is keen to stress that Jesus is about to speak rabbinically, so he uses this standard Jewish expression that Jesus 'sat down'. Matthew wants us to know that here is a rabbi addressing us and that he is about to deliver something important to those who wish to be his disciples. Listen carefully if you want to follow him.

Matthew repeats this idea of Jesus sitting to teach at two other points in his gospel. In Matthew 13:1-2 Jesus is by Lake Galilee and we read that he 'got into a boat and sat in it', in order to teach the large crowds who had gathered on the shore. Then in Matthew 24:3, in Jesus' final discourse to his disciples on the important topic of his return at the end of the age, we find him 'sitting on the Mount of Olives' while his disciples come to him privately for instruction.

Altogether these three statements of Jesus sitting to teach herald three of the five big teaching blocks which Matthew employs to get across the main messages of Jesus. These three sections are interspersed with two others (chapters 10 and 18). In the first of these, significantly, Jesus sends out his disciples to do what he has been doing. This is the next part of their apprenticeship and, as we have seen, a key component of discipleship.

Go and make disciples

All this is heading towards a climax in Matthew's Gospel where Jesus instructs his remaining eleven disciples to 'go and make disciples of all nations' (Matt. 28:19). Again, this was typical of first-century Judaism. Disciples became teachers who made more disciples. However, once more, there are significant differences in Jesus' case.

Let us make two points to start with. First, the occasion of Matthew 28:19 was not the same as that of the ascension which took place just outside Jerusalem, whereas the setting of what we call the Great Commission was in Galilee. Here, Jesus was not just about to leave them. In fact, it may have been one of the early resurrection appearances.

Secondly, the simple statement 'go and make' has given rise to a lot of debate. Is this a double imperative, meaning that both verbs take the form of commands? In which case, to be fully obedient to the Great Commission requires being sent somewhere specific before any disciple-making can take place. Pack your bags and set off.

But some point out that in this statement there is really only one command, namely 'make', as the verb 'go' is in a middle voice which is reflexive and not an imperative. This sounds rather technical, but basically it means that 'go' is more like a participle, based on a word derived from 'piercing' or 'going through', and so should be translated in other ways, such as 'in your going' or 'as you are going'. This means you are to make disciples as you go about your normal life, wherever you go. Of course, the apostles being addressed here would be sent out into all nations, 'to the ends of the earth' (Acts 1:8), but for most of us Matthew 28:19 is not a missionary call as such. Long-distance travel is not essential. Opportunities to make disciples are all around you, wherever you go.

To be fair, opinions remain divided on the grammar of Jesus' statement in Matthew 28:19. Some insist that when a participle like this is attached to an imperative in this way it becomes 'attendant' upon it and therefore also takes the form of a command. The less technical term is that it 'piggybacks' the second verb, creating a double command in the process! Apparently, there are other examples of this type of construction which bear this out but this is getting beyond our scope. Those who are familiar with the Greek language can weigh up the arguments but for the rest of us, we can simply accept both interpretations! Some believers must go somewhere at the Lord's command, just as the original disciples had to. For others, it is sufficient to make disciples 'as we go through life', wherever life takes us.

Whichever is correct for us, the main point remains: disciples make more disciples. That is an essential part of discipleship. But what is crucial here is once again the matter of authority. A rabbi usually passed on his authority to a handful of his disciples, especially in preparation for when he was no longer with them. But in these verses Jesus makes it clear he is not doing that. In Matthew 28:18, Jesus declares that 'All authority in heaven and on earth has been given to me'. And, it seems, it remains with him. He is not passing it on. Why? Because he is still alive, *and will be forever*. So rather than handing over this authority, he instead gives them the promise that 'I am with you always, to the very end of the age' (Matt. 28:20). They *are* to make more disciples but under *his* authority, not their own.

With this in mind, an earlier verse in Matthew may now make more sense: 'Nor are you to be called 'teacher', for you have one Teacher, the Christ' (Matt. 23:10; see also verse 8 of this chapter where the same applies to not being called 'Rabbi'). But surely the disciples are to become teachers? Isn't that what Jesus is wanting in his commission at the end of the gospel? Didn't all rabbis want this of their disciples?

Certainly, but usually when a disciple was fully trained he then raised up his own disciples, and became the rabbi and father to this new generation (if you recall, father-son was another way of expressing the rabbi-disciple relationship). It is this that Jesus forbids. He did not want a series of new 'schools', that of Peter, of John, and so on. They were not to raise up disciples to *themselves*, rather they were to make more for *him*, the one who remained their teacher forever.

This is the second main difference between Jesus and the other rabbis of the time. He retains his authority because he was raised from the dead and lives forever. That is also why the disciples were to pass on his teaching, and in particular teach others to obey what Jesus had commanded them (Matt. 28:20). All future disciples would have to learn to do what Jesus said, not just memorise his words.

This is how discipleship should still work today. We are to find those who are willing to accept Jesus as their rabbi and become like him. That is how to fulfil the commission he has left us. When we make such disciples under his authority, then we can be sure he is with us.

Teachers, or indeed any leaders, are not to create their own followers. Inevitably this happens to some extent, but that is not to be the aim and can become a problem. Isn't this what was happening at Corinth, something that Paul had to oppose? In 1 Corinthians 1:12 Paul writes, 'One of you says, "I follow Paul"; another, "I follow Apollos"; another, "I follow Cephas"; still another, "I follow Christ."' It would appear that those within the church at Corinth were attaching themselves to particular teachers or leaders as their followers or disciples. It is no surprise, therefore, that division and confusion was occurring. But how easy it is for a leader to want their own following! It satisfies an innate desire for self-aggrandisement and admiration. Moreover, we all like to have human leaders that suit us and to follow them, even if sometimes that is instead of Jesus himself.

Those of us who are teachers within the church must realise we do not have any authority of our own. We have no other option but to teach under his authority. We need to be constantly aware of this and understand that his authority is not just something that applied when he was teaching on earth. It remains for us, and for all time. He is the only Teacher that heaven has fully accredited.

For this reason, we are not to teach anything new from ourselves. We must teach from the whole Bible, always keeping in mind everything Jesus taught and that he remains our rabbi. This is the case whether we are teaching from his own scriptures (what we call the Old Testament) or from the New Testament. We are quite safe in this latter case as we can be confident that all the apostles knew they had to teach under the authority of Jesus. We have already seen that Paul said, 'Follow me as I follow Christ' (1 Cor. 4:15-16, 11:1), meaning that Jesus was Paul's rabbi even though he had never been with Jesus during his earthly ministry.

We have covered quite a lot of ground in these opening pages but it has been important in order to stress that the teachings we will be studying are those of our rabbi *today*. These are not just things he said in the past to a Jewish audience. Moreover, if we are to pass on his teaching faithfully, it has to be under his authority. And we can't do that unless we are following him wholeheartedly as modern disciples. To that end we need to listen carefully to the Jewish Jesus.

With all this in mind, we are ready to start examining some of Jesus' teaching. In our next chapter we will begin with a short but important passage in Luke, still on the theme of discipleship.

Chapter Three

No Excuses!

Luke 9:57-62

In this chapter we are going to study the above passage, so take time to read through this now and then keep it open in front of you.

In previous chapters we have seen that becoming a disciple, especially of Jesus, was not something to be taken up lightly. There was nothing insubstantial or trivial about a calling of this kind. In fact, it could be very costly. It often involved leaving relatives and friends, and travelling around the country. The total commitment required meant that any prospective disciple first had to be sure his priorities were in order.

Here in this passage, Luke has put together three short incidents to highlight this. The only other gospel writer to include these examples is Matthew, and he records only two of them (Matt. 8:18-21). It doesn't matter to us whether or not all three occurred straight after each other on the same day. Perhaps this is unlikely but we can assume that they shared a similar setting, namely 'As they were walking along the road' (Luke 9:57). We can also be sure that Luke has deliberately set them side by side to illustrate the same point, namely the cost of following Jesus.

Before we look at the individual components, it is instructive to consider the structure of the whole passage. Here we have three events with two verses for each. This tripartite form is quite typical within the gospel accounts, being designed to reinforce the overall message while allowing for some variation.

A passage of this kind lends itself to a certain amount of analysis. It is worth taking some time to look through these verses for yourself and ask certain questions. What are the similarities between the three incidents? And what differences stand out? Read these verses slowly, or even write them out for yourself, or underline key words or phrases. See what you can find before reading on.

All three components of this passage are tied together in certain ways. The words 'follow' and 'go' are common to all of them, and each ends with a rather cryptic remark from Jesus to explain the cost or challenge of following him. He uses images from the outdoor world, nature and farming, or from the customs of the day. Some of these might seem strange to us. That is the clue that there is something Hebraic about his statements, and that we need to listen carefully to the Jewish Jesus.

Then there are further similarities within two of the three episodes while the remaining one is different. For instance, in the first and third the man is volunteering, whereas in the second he is being recruited. The first man is willing to follow and go, but has not considered the cost. The second man is asked to follow, but wants to do something first. The third man, similar to the first, wants to follow but he is like the second in that he has a 'but first', which also involves his family.

As another example, each of the outer pair is constructed as a simple two-statement dialogue: the man, then Jesus. However, the middle dialogue has three statements: Jesus, the man, then Jesus again, making it slightly more complex.

Despite several similarities between the first and third episodes, they are not identical. There is a progression. The first man offers to follow unconditionally but is challenged to consider the cost. The third man seems to have done this but he has a very specific condition.

These similarities and repetitions bind the whole passage together into a threefold narrative, but the differences highlight that each individual must respond to the challenge of discipleship in his own way.

A final point is that the second and third episodes are linked by another feature. We have already noticed the common 'first let me' as each of these men pleads to return home and deal with family affairs before following Jesus. Perhaps for this reason they also both end with Jesus referring to the kingdom of God. Implied here is a contrast between their existing lives and the new one that is on offer now that Jesus is among them.

Let us now examine the individual dialogues in turn, in particular to get a better understanding of their distinctively Hebraic nature.

Laying your head

In the first case, someone approaches Jesus as he is walking along the road, presumably with his disciples, most likely teaching them as they go along. The man seems to be drawn into the situation and shows an interest in joining them. But Jesus recognises there is something shallow in his understanding of what this would mean and has to enlighten him. But how well have we grasped what Jesus is telling him?

Typically, we have been told from Luke 9:58 that this means Jesus had nowhere to stay at night, taking the phrase 'lay his head' to have something to do with sleeping. Our English usage can mislead us. We might say, 'I'm going to lay my head down', presumably on a soft pillow in a nice warm bed. So we conclude that Jesus had no bed for the night and often had to sleep rough, perhaps in the fields or by the roadside. From this we readily deduce that he was poor and had a tough life. Anyone following him would have to accept this way of life and be prepared for such hardships.

This interpretation runs into several difficulties. Firstly, such a scenario is totally out of keeping with the nature of Middle Eastern hospitality, which would never allow anyone to spend the night without a roof over his head, let alone an esteemed and popular itinerant teacher such as Jesus. He would have been welcomed almost anywhere in Galilee. Even when he visited the more hostile Jerusalem, he still had somewhere nearby to stay, with Mary, Martha and Lazarus at Bethany, for instance.

Moreover, Jesus and his disciples did not wander about destitute. They were supported by several relatively wealthy ladies (Luke 8:1-3) and they had a money bag so full it seems that Judas reckoned he could dip his hand into it without anyone noticing much was missing (John 12:6, 13:29).

The second clue that we have misunderstood what Jesus is saying is found in his own illustration of birds and foxes. Birds do not usually sleep in nests; when they want to sleep, they roost, usually in trees. They build nests only at certain times and for a different purpose altogether, namely to lay eggs in readiness for birth and to feed the newly hatched baby birds until they are mature and able to fly. Similarly, foxes sleep in dens, not holes. They build holes for another reason. Like birds with their nests, they aim to create a safe place in which to give birth and look after their young until they are ready to fend for themselves. Of course, they may sleep in these holes during this period but that is not the primary purpose of a fox's hole, or indeed of a bird's nest.

These two illustrations from nature fit perfectly the true meaning of Jesus having 'nowhere to lay his head'. The Hebrew phrase 'to lay one's head' is a specific idiom related to teaching, not sleeping. It refers to passing on instruction. Teaching is about sharing what you know, taking the knowledge and thoughts that are in your head and transferring them to someone else's. At least that is the aim. Many students have wished this was a simple download rather than a prolonged and arduous process!

Remember that in this passage Jesus is responding to someone who has said he will 'follow' him, meaning he wants to become Jesus' disciple and so learn from him. Also recall that the rabbi-disciple relationship is regarded as being like a father bringing up sons. So Jesus is talking here about his function as a rabbi, that of reproducing his teaching in his 'sons'. But unlike the birds and foxes he doesn't have a nest or hole in which to do this. What does this mean in this context?

The use of the phrase 'nowhere to lay his head' quite possibly refers to the fact that Jesus doesn't have a specific place where he does his teaching. There is no formal 'school' where he holds classes. In Matthew's Gospel we are told that this would-be disciple was himself a teacher of the Law (Matt. 8:19). As such he may have been used to having a regular place to teach and expected that Jesus would operate in the same way. He needed to be told that Jesus didn't hold classes for a couple of hours twice a week, for instance. True discipling involved far more. Was he prepared for that?

Another aspect to the phrase 'lay his head' may indicate that Jesus is looking for those on whom he can 'place his headship'. The head is functional: it tells the rest of the body what to do. In looking for somewhere to 'lay his head', Jesus is stressing that being his disciple is not just about physically following him around, but allowing his teaching to control every aspect of your life. He is challenging the young man, 'Is that what you mean when you say you will follow me wherever? Will you let me lay my head on you in everything you do?'

This simple example helps us realise that we need to listen to the Jewish Jesus properly if we don't want to miss the main point of his teaching. While there may indeed have been physical hardships in travelling around as a disciple of Jesus, that is not what this verse is telling us. We are beginning to see that reading a text without the necessary

Hebraic background can create many misconceptions and lead us down false paths. Let's see what the next dialogue has to offer.

Burying the dead

This conversation is with someone who has shown no initial interest in following Jesus but who has been picked out as a possible disciple. Jesus initiates the dialogue and ends it with an emphatic command to the would-be follower to begin his life as a disciple now. In the Greek, the 'you' is emphasised in such a way as to suggest it should be repeated, as in 'as for you, you go' (Luke 9:60).

But It is the first part of Jesus' response ('Let the dead bury their own dead') that is mystifying, and seemingly rather harsh. That is because we assume that the man's father is already dead or dying, and that Jesus shrugs this off as of no consequence. But the opposite is true. The father is very much alive, and the son is making an excuse to avoid taking up Jesus' command to follow him.

The key to a better understanding is to realise that 'to bury one's father' is a Hebraic idiom that refers to the duty of the son to remain at home and care for his parents until they are laid to rest. So the man's comment, 'First let me go and bury my father', means his father is still alive and may well be for some years. Implied in his statement is 'I'll go home for now but when he dies and my family duties are over, then I'll think about following you.'

Basically he intends to defer the matter to a distant future when his father dies as an old man. This is a delaying device, putting the pressure back on Jesus. 'There are certain strong family demands upon me which surely you can't expect me to ignore, can you?' Yet Jesus did. His call to discipleship overrides family ties. Let the dead (those with no interest in the kingdom or following Jesus) deal with such matters. The prospective disciple is called to start a new father-son relationship.

The fact that this conversation takes place 'on the road' backs up this scenario. If his father had just died then the young man should have been at home observing the seven-day period of mourning called *shivah*. During this time family members were not allowed to leave the house as others came to pay their respects. And if his father was dying, he would again have been expected to be at home.

It is interesting to note that the idiom is still in use in Jewish circles today. 'Aren't you going to bury your father first?' might be asked of someone who had plans that involved moving away from their family.

Also a father might say to one of his sons, 'I want you to bury me.' The chosen son is not expected to find a shovel and start digging a hole, rather to recognise that this will be his duty in the future. Moreover, if the father did not have any sons, or regarded them as unworthy, he might ask another young person to take this on. 'I hope you will be the one to bury me' would be taken to mean 'I look upon you as a son and ask that you will one day lay me to rest'.

While all this provides a satisfactory explanation for the dialogue, there is an alternative which is worth knowing about. In this scenario the young man is between two burials. Jewish tradition required the body to be placed in the ground on the day of death. This was the first burial. The family then observed the weeklong *shivah*.

A year later, on the first anniversary of the death, when the flesh had wasted away, the bones were collected and placed in a small chest called an ossuary. This was done by the oldest son who placed the ossuary next to their ancestors, perhaps in a family burial cave. This was called the secondary burial, a practice which became popular in the first century but which is no longer done.

Perhaps this man was between these two burials. The first could have happened up to a year earlier, so he would not still be in the period of mourning, but he wanted to perform the second burial before following Jesus. In which case, Jesus here was not approving the secondary burial as it had no scriptural basis. Moreover, there had developed a superstition that the decomposition of the flesh between the two burials atoned for the sins of the dead person. Jesus would definitely be against that!

This second option might account for Jesus' tough words to the man, but overall it is less preferable to the explanation involving an idiomatic expression. Either way, the man was making an excuse. And when it comes to following Jesus, there are no excuses!

Saying good-bye

The third dialogue, like the first, involves a volunteer, but one with a precondition. It is usually translated along the lines of, 'Let me first go back home and say farewell to my folks.' This seems reasonable. Wasn't Elisha allowed to do the same (1 Kgs 19:20)? So again, why is Jesus taking a hard line?

Our understanding is again obscured by translation. The Greek *apotasso* can mean 'say good-bye', but, more usually, conveys the idea of 'taking leave' of someone. The distinction is important in the culture of the time. The person who is leaving must request permission to leave from those who are staying. Meanwhile, it is those remaining behind who say good-bye to those who are leaving. This was a polite formality observed all over the Middle East. It is not for you simply to say good-bye and leave; you ask to leave, then (if agreed) good-bye – as in 'God be with you' or 'God go with you' – is said to you.

Here the potential disciple is asking to go and get permission from those at home. Everyone listening knew what he meant, and that in all likelihood his father would refuse to let him go off on some seemingly questionable venture. This gives the man a ready-made excuse. He can insist he will follow, knowing that he won't be allowed to!

He is saying, 'I will follow you, but the authority of my father is higher and I must have his permission first.' Jesus is saying, 'My authority is higher.' This seems shocking, until we realise once again that the rabbi-disciple relationship resembled that of father and son.

Jesus indicates his disapproval of the young man's excuse with a response from the world of agriculture. He talks of putting your hand (not hands) to the plough. The light plough used then was guided with just one hand, usually the left. This was to keep it upright, regulate its depth by pressure and lift it over any stones. The other hand was used to drive the oxen with a goad, an iron spike about two yards long. At the same time the ploughman had to keep his eyes on the furrow by looking intensely between the hind quarters of the oxen.

This all needed dexterity and concentration. To look round could be disastrous. A distracted ploughman might catch the plough on a rock and break it, or cut back into a previously ploughed furrow and destroy what had already been done. Or he might cut aimlessly into unploughed ground and make future work more difficult. His job was to work in harmony with the labour already done and that still to be done. In the service of the kingdom, anything other than complete dedication and focus could be not only unproductive but actually destructive.

You are the man!

Two further points remain to be made about this passage overall. In each case the man is not named. His identity remains unknown. Why is this? Because he is you, and me! His anonymity means we can put ourselves in these situations and ask, 'Are these our excuses?' Do we put off following Jesus fully for reasons like these? What would our response be if we heard Jesus talking to us like that? These stories are not about naming and shaming three particular individuals, but are recorded to warn and challenge us.

And that's the other key point. We are not told the outcome in any of the three incidents. The men do not speak again. Jesus has the last word. But it would be wrong to assume they all turned away and never followed him. Who knows?

Each story is left suspended. Why is this? So that we might complete the conversation with our own response.

Let's end by considering a similar situation in which another young man approached Jesus to ask about eternal life (Matt. 19:16-22, Mark 10:17-22, Luke 18:18-25). Again, we don't know his name, just that he was well-meaning and Torah observant. Later we learn that he had great wealth and that he went away sad. From this we assume that he must have rejected Jesus' words. But not necessarily. He might equally have been sad because he was going to do exactly what Jesus had said! Again the story is left without a full ending. If this nameless man was you, what would you have done?

So we've seen there is a cost to following Jesus, and much of it seems to do with the family. But we haven't finished with this theme yet, as we will see in our next chapter.

Chapter Four

It's All Relative

Luke 14:26

In this chapter we will continue to look at what it means to be a disciple of Jesus, and in particular focus on what Jesus says in Luke 14:26. This verse has often puzzled readers in that it seems incredibly harsh and most unlike Jesus. 'If anyone comes to me and does not hate father and mother, wife and children, brothers and sisters – yes, even life itself – such a person cannot be my disciple.'

How can Jesus make hating other members of your family a necessary condition of discipleship? Moreover, doesn't it contradict other scriptures? For instance, one of the Ten Commandments tells us to honour our father and mother (Exod. 20:12) and later in the New Testament Paul exhorts husbands to love their wives (Eph. 5:25, 28). We have seen that the cost of being a disciple of Jesus is high, but isn't this going too far?

There is a parallel passage in Matthew which helps to clarify this a little. In Matthew 10:37 we don't find the word 'hate'. Instead Jesus says that loving family members *'more than me'* is what makes us unworthy of being his disciple.

Some may be bothered by the apparent discrepancies between these two gospel accounts. In English they don't seem to match up. For instance, it is possible to love your wife more than your cat without this meaning you hate your pet. There must be something more going on in the text than we realise.

The key point is that in this context, love and hate are not emotions but preferences. This is about choices, and as such is a matter of the will rather than the heart. In Hebraic terms, to love means to put first, and to hate means to put second. It's all relative!

We see this in other scriptures. In Malachi 1:2-3 God declares, 'I have loved Jacob, but Esau I have hated.' This is not an emotional reaction by God towards these twin brothers, rather he is reiterating his covenant choice. Even though Esau was born first, it was Jacob whom God put first when renewing the covenant previously made with Abraham and Isaac (see Genesis chapters 28 and 35). Esau had to take second place as it was through Jacob that God would work out his plans and promises. It is within this context that the love-hate statement plays out.

In another interesting passage we learn that Leah was the 'hated' wife of Jacob (Gen. 29:31). At least that is what the Hebrew actually says, and certain translations do adhere to this, for instance the King James Version and English Standard Version. Others, such as the New International Version, rework it as 'Leah was not loved', which might seem better but is not strictly accurate. Leah *was* loved, just not as much as Rachel was. We see this in Genesis 29:30 where we read that Jacob's love for Rachel was *greater* than his love for Leah. In effect, Leah took second place in Jacob's affections. It is in that sense, in Hebraic thinking, that she was 'hated'.

We meet this again in Deuteronomy 21:15-17, a passage primarily about the rights of the firstborn and what might happen if a man has two wives, one loved and the other 'hated'. The problem being resolved here is that if the firstborn is the son of the 'hated' one, then the husband must accept that and not give the rights of the firstborn to the first son of the 'loved' one. Again, our translations may well tell us incorrectly that the two wives are loved and *not loved*, the English language struggling to cope with the Hebraic concept of 'hated' in this context. But as before, the point is simply that one is loved more than the other, and that in this tricky *ménage à trois* the personal preferences of the husband must not override God's law concerning the firstborn.

A similar thought lies behind Jesus' statement in Matthew 6:24 that 'No-one can serve two masters.' Or at least, not equally. One will be loved more than the other, which is expressed as 'you will hate the one and love the other' (Matt. 6:24). Here the idiom is being applied to God and Mammon (worldly wealth and possessions). Incidentally, this was the predicament of the rich young man we mentioned in our previous chapter (Matt. 19:16-22). He was trying to love both when he needed to learn how to hate!

So now we realise that Hebraically, 'hate' can be used to mean 'love less' or 'put second'. But that doesn't reduce the degree of commitment required to follow Jesus, especially when it comes to family relationships. Here's another intriguing incident to ponder.

One busy day when Jesus was teaching the crowds, his mother and brothers arrived hoping to see him, or at least have a word with him (Matt. 12:46-50, Mark 3:31-35, Luke 8:20-21). The text doesn't say what they wanted to talk to Jesus about but because of the crowds they couldn't get close and had to stand outside. When someone told Jesus about this he responded by pointing to his disciples and saying, 'Here are my mother and my brothers' (Matt. 12:49), adding that whoever does the will of the Father in heaven is to be considered as his family.

This is often seen as being rather disrespectful to his actual mother and brothers, but we shouldn't assume this, or that he was ignoring them. He may well have gone outside to talk to them fairly quickly, or even welcomed them in. Nor was he necessarily excluding them from his 'wider family'. It all depended on whether they were also committed to his heavenly Father.

However, what *was* happening in this passage is that Jesus was doing what any rabbi would do in these circumstances. He took advantage of the situation to teach! The unexpected arrival of his relatives meant that an opportunity had arisen to make a simple point before bringing his teaching to a conclusion. Rabbis always looked around to find examples and illustrations that were at hand. What Jesus said on this occasion was for the benefit of the disciples there, something positive for them to grasp, not something negative to discredit his family. Incidentally, notice how Jesus pointed to his disciples while making his comment about them. Again, this was typical of a rabbinic style of teaching, intended to reinforce the message.

We might ask whether Mary completely understood what Jesus was saying here. We may hope so. But perhaps her perspective was still rather limited and it was all a little confusing for her. This idea of Jesus having a bigger family may have created a real tension, especially among his brothers who as yet did not believe that Jesus was the Messiah. Indeed, we may also wonder what the mothers of the other disciples felt about 'losing' their sons to the Jesus mission. His disciples may have been told they would be well rewarded for leaving all to follow him, but what about those they had left behind in order to do so?

In the case of Mary it all ended happily. Even while in agony on the cross, Jesus made sure that after his death Mary would be looked after by the apostle John, when he said to her, 'Woman, here is your son,' and to John, 'Here is your mother' (John 19:26-27).

The bigger family was now working in her favour. Moreover, his mother and his brothers too were all eventually fully part of what Jesus had started. We read in Acts 1:14 that after his ascension they regularly joined the other apostles for prayer. We can assume they were also part of the hundred and twenty believers mentioned in Acts 1:15 and would go on to experience the power of the Holy Spirit at Pentecost (Acts 2:1-4).

But what about the wife of a disciple? How might she fare when her husband committed himself to a rabbi? Although most disciples were young, some might already have married as marriage tended to take place at an early age (often around eighteen years old). Peter, for instance, was certainly married as we read he had a mother-in-law whom Jesus healed (Matt. 8:14-15).

There is an interesting passage on this matter in the Mishnah, a major collection of the oral traditions of the time of Jesus which was later written down around the start of the second century AD. In one of the tractates of the Mishnah we learn that a disciple could be absent from home for up to thirty days to study with a rabbi, even against the will of his wife (Ketubot 5:6). After that, he needed her permission!

Another part of the Mishnah illustrates that in certain cases your rabbi was to be esteemed above your own father. If both your father and your rabbi have lost something or both are bearing a burden, then you should attend to the needs of your rabbi first. And if both are taken captive, then you are to ransom your rabbi first and your father second! A good example of 'hating', even if it isn't that clear today what 'taken captive' and 'ransom' might mean! There was one exception in all these cases. If your father was also a teacher then you could put him first. Otherwise he came second as he only brought you into this world, while your rabbi was giving you wisdom that would bring you into the world to come (Baba Metzia 2:11).

If some of this still seems shocking to us, it is only because we have not yet fully appreciated the significance of the rabbi-disciple relationship of the time. You could not be halfway in. Moreover, the father-son aspect of discipleship, which we have already discussed, was seen as a great privilege based on a long tradition, probably dating as far back as the time of Elijah. In 2 Kings we see that Elijah was training up many younger prophets. Although this is often translated differently, for instance 'the company of the prophets' (2 Kgs 2:3, 5, 7, 15), the Hebrew is actually 'sons of the prophets'. This idea is also seen in 2 Kings 2:12 where Elisha, one of Elijah's disciples, calls out to Elijah, 'My father! My father!'

We cannot leave our verse in Luke about a disciple 'hating' his own family members without commenting that Jesus also adds 'yes, even life itself' (or, in some translations, 'yes, even his own life'). Again it must be made clear that Jesus is not telling us to engage in self-loathing or to count our lives as worthless, rather to put ourselves and our own self-interests second to the demands of discipleship.

Another point is worth making on this whole matter of cutting free from previous family ties in order to pursue the life of a disciple. Our character, personality, habits and attitudes are initially formed amongst immediate family members – father and mother, brothers and sisters. Such an umbilical cord of attachment may not help in submitting to a rabbi who is expected to create disciples in imitation of himself. Indeed, such previous relationships may deflect us from our new path. It may be necessary to renounce their ways and cut off their influence, but this is not to be done with a sense of literal hating. A loving and honouring relationship with our families can be maintained even while we allow Jesus to shape our lives differently.

Finally in this chapter, let us consider the words of Jesus to Peter at the end of John's Gospel, when he says to his disciple, 'Do you love me more than these?' (John 21:15). Some say that *these* refers to the other disciples, presumably meaning 'do you love me more than these love me', rather than 'do you love me more than you love them'! This explanation is offered on the basis of Peter's earlier boast that he would never fall away even if all the other disciples did, implying that his love for Jesus was greater than theirs (Matt. 26:33, Mark 14:29). Peter's humble response indicates that he has learned that lesson and would never make such claims again.

However, some suggest an alternative scenario. Instead Jesus is referring to the fishing business that Peter has returned to. In which case *these* must be the fish or the boats. If only we had been there we might have seen where Jesus was pointing!

But even if we can't sort out this conundrum for sure, one thing is certain. If Peter had not replied, 'Yes, Lord', then we could conclude that he 'hated' Jesus!

There is more on the theme of discipleship to be drawn from this poignant ending to John's Gospel, but for that we need to reflect on one of the darker aspects of the gospel story, which is the subject of our next chapter – betrayal!

Chapter Five

Betrayal!

Matthew 26:20-25, John 18:17, 25

We ended the last chapter by saying that the subject of our next one would be that of betrayal. Whenever the betrayal of Jesus is mentioned, one name automatically comes to mind – Judas! This is common knowledge, even to those outside of the Christian faith. Everyone identifies this disciple as the perpetrator of this treacherous act. Nor is this surprising, as it is so clearly set out in the gospels.

At the Last Supper, Jesus announces that he will be betrayed and indicates which of the Twelve the traitor will be (Matt. 26:20-25). But we don't need to wait until this moment to discover his identity. Time and again when Judas is mentioned in the gospels we are told that he 'was later to betray him' (John 6:71, 12:4). Judas is constantly being referred to in this way (see Mark 14:10, Luke 22:4, John 18:2, 5).

Even more curious is that earlier in the gospels, in the list of those Jesus chose as his apostles, we find the big spoiler that Judas is 'the traitor' (Luke 6:16) or the one 'who betrayed him' (Matt. 10:4, Mark 3:19). Why give this away so early and so often? Might we otherwise miss it?!

So the mystery is not so much 'whodunnit?' but why. Given what we have already learnt about the rabbi-disciple relationship, how can a disciple, *any* disciple, have acted against his rabbi in this way? However, some claim this wasn't the *only* act of betrayal recorded in the gospels. What if this happened not once but *twice*, and there were two different culprits, one of whom is less overtly flagged up in advance? This needs investigating!

Firstly, it is worth noting how, at the Last Supper, when Jesus startled his disciples by talking of his betrayal, Judas (even at this stage in the text still being referred to as 'the one who would betray him') asked, 'Surely not I, Rabbi?' and has to be told, 'Yes, it is you' (Matt. 26:25). And this is even after he had already visited the chief priests and made financial arrangements to 'hand Jesus over' to them, another way of describing the act of betrayal (Matt. 26:14-16).

Judas' reaction to Jesus' statement seems one of genuine surprise – perhaps he hadn't read the earlier chapters of the gospels yet! Or, more likely, perhaps he did not consider that what he was about to do constituted a betrayal. It has been put forward by way of an explanation for his actions that Judas had misread Jesus' intentions. All the disciples misunderstood to some extent, but Judas more so, and to greater consequence. He saw the confrontation that was developing between Jesus and the authorities and, misguided, he tried to force Jesus' hand and kick-start the revolt he believed Jesus had planned. In Judas' mind this was not a betrayal, but an attempt to bring to a head what had been planned all along. He was helping out his rabbi.

This also, it is suggested, explains why he felt so guilty afterwards when a revolt did not transpire. Once he saw that Jesus didn't fight back and was condemned to death, Judas (the text still hammering it home even after the event that it was he 'who had betrayed him'!) was seized with remorse and confessed that he had sinned and betrayed innocent blood (Matt. 27:3).

Of course, we cannot ignore the fact that Judas had been prompted by Satan to betray Jesus (John 13:2), nor that his betrayal had been predicted and was inevitable within God's overall plan. There are mysteries and debates here that could occupy us for ages! But let us leave Judas for a moment and turn our attention to another act of betrayal, one not heralded beforehand and one we do usually miss, even though it would not have escaped a Jewish reader at the time.

Who is this other betrayer? None other than the prime apostle, Peter himself. We all know that Peter denied Jesus but it was far more serious than we usually understand. Admittedly, in Matthew's account the word is 'disown' not 'deny' (Matt. 26:34), which may add to the gravity of the incident, but this still does not go far enough. What we call a denial, a Jewish reader would regard as a betrayal. How is this?

John's account brings the answer out best. Whereas in the other gospels Peter is challenged with simply being 'with' Jesus or 'one of them', the wording in John is more pointed: 'You aren't one of this man's *disciples* too, are you?' (John 18:17, 25, italics mine). His reply is emphatic: 'I am not.'

What we can miss here is that Peter was not just denying a friendship or the fact that he knew Jesus; rather, he was publicly disassociating himself from his rabbi. This was more than a denial. It was tantamount to a betrayal.

As we have seen, there was a very close bond between a rabbi and his disciples, closer than family ties. The rabbi was totally committed to his disciples and they, by accepting his call, were completely dedicated to him. For three years, Peter's identity and whole life had been bound up in such a relationship and it meant everything.

That's why when Peter realised what he had done he wasn't just a little upset. Rather, he went out and wept bitterly (Matt. 26:75). For him, it had wrecked everything. The consequences were severe. It meant he could no longer be considered a disciple of Jesus. Disowning him in this way was the worst insult you could give to your rabbi. Judas had made his error but, in Peter's mind, what he had done was much worse. Refusing to associate with your rabbi, especially at his time of greatest need, was a deeper betrayal. There was no coming back from this, so Peter believed. Moreover, the other disciples and followers would think the same.

With this in mind, Mark 16:7 takes on a new meaning. At the empty tomb on resurrection morning the angel delivered a message to the women which began: 'But go, tell his disciples *and Peter* . . .' (italics mine). Why is Peter singled out here? Was it because Peter was no longer regarded as a disciple, at least by those the angel was addressing? Perhaps the angel mentioned Peter separately as otherwise the women would have told the other disciples but not him. We may assume Peter would have found out eventually, but here is a hint that he was no longer included in the circle of disciples, at least in the minds of others.

All of this makes John chapter 21 even more poignant and powerful. We refer to this as 'the restoration of Peter', but we can only fully understand the nature of this restoration when we have seen what had been broken previously. Only John records this incident, and it is important for what follows in Acts. Without it, the opening of Acts wouldn't make sense. Here is Peter back among the disciples, leading the way, preaching to the crowds. How has that happened?

In John chapter 21, Peter has gone back to what he knows best, fishing, still believing that he doesn't really belong with the other disciples now. He has betrayed his rabbi, and even though Jesus is now back from the dead and being seen by them, Peter's offence rules him out from ever being a disciple again.

Then Jesus appears on the shore.

The scene is well known: the multitude of fish, the fire of burning coals reminiscent of the one which kept Peter warm during his betrayal, and the breakfast together. All the time Peter is aware of the fractured relationship that remains.

Then comes Jesus' threefold questioning of Peter and Peter's responses, which we briefly looked at in the previous chapter. This passage is a gift to preachers as they unpack the meaning of the words and Peter's feelings of hurt as the same question comes for the third time, reminding him of his threefold denial. We can imagine Jesus and Peter now walking together along the shore some distance from the others as Jesus lovingly restores and recommissions him.

But the key words are often missed: two simple but vital words. 'Follow me!' (John 21:19). Here was something

Peter knew from before (see Matt. 4:19). This was the call to discipleship he was familiar with. Perhaps he could hardly believe his ears, but when this was reiterated shortly afterwards with the words, 'You must follow me' (John 21:22), Peter knew he could be a disciple again.

Meanwhile, Judas was no longer there. His story had ended differently. While Peter went out and wept bitterly, Judas went away and hanged himself (Matt. 27:5). Judas saw no tomorrow, no hope. In that sense, his betrayal went further than facilitating Jesus' arrest, and was worse than that of Peter. By taking his own life, he was denying everything his rabbi had taught about forgiveness, about loving those who hate you and about God's mercy to those who truly repent.

Would Jesus have forgiven Judas and restored him too? We might consider it unlikely, given what we know about the story as a whole, but can we really be sure? Judas obviously didn't believe it was possible. He didn't give Jesus a chance to restore him.

In the end, Judas' betrayal was not just about thirty pieces of silver or a kiss in the garden. It was a betrayal of what his rabbi had taught him. On the other hand, Peter still trusted what his rabbi had said, even when he thought his discipleship was over. He had listened more carefully and taken it to heart. Somehow it stayed with him in his deepest despair.

Overall, there is much to be gained from studying both betrayals and comparing them. Moreover, when we place these familiar events within the context of a first-century rabbi-disciple relationship we begin to understand them so much better.

It is also worth noticing that Jesus not only knew about both in advance, but he predicted them in such a way that both Peter and Judas, as well as the other disciples, would realise that he knew. Do we find it reassuring that Jesus knows what we are like before we do?

In addition, we learn that Jesus had prayed for Peter that his faith would not fail (Luke 22:32). Without this prayer, might Peter, like Judas, have also given up completely and ended his life in despair? But Jesus had interceded for Peter so that he would turn back and then be able to strengthen the other disciples, something else that should reassure us.

Now that his discipleship had been restored, Peter could become that rock on which Jesus declared that he would build his church (Matt. 16:18). But what did Jesus mean by this statement and others in the same passage? Here is another passage which creates a lot of debate and confusion. In our next chapter we will listen carefully to the Jewish Jesus as 'he opened his mouth and spoke' these words.

Chapter Six

What's in a Name?

Matthew 16:17-19

Our task in this chapter is to probe into one of the most Hebraic passages of the New Testament, namely Matthew 16:17-19. In just a few verses we meet several biblical and rabbinic references, and are faced with a complex set of ideas and allusions. All this stems from Peter's important confession that Jesus is 'the Messiah, the Son of the Living God' (Matt. 16:16). This realisation had not emerged from anything previously taught by any man (the phrase in v. 17, 'flesh and blood', is an idiomatic way of referring to mankind). Rather, it was a revelation directly from the Father in heaven. Jesus recognised this immediately for Peter did not merely declare his rabbi to be the longed-for Messiah, but also the 'Son of the Living God', or as in another gospel, *'God's* Messiah' (Luke 9:20), also sometimes translated as 'the Christ *of God'* (italics mine).

This was a fresh perception and indicated the supernatural origin of Peter's disclosure. Much would change as a result of this defining moment, but first Jesus spoke personally to Peter in the earshot of the other disciples. Let's also listen in to what the Jewish Jesus had to say to him.

The remarks Jesus made in Matthew 16:17-19 have stirred much debate and controversy and have also led to a lot of misunderstanding. Some of this surrounds the name change of the disciple from Simon to Peter and the reasons behind it. It is well known that there was wordplay involved when Jesus used 'Peter' and 'rock' in the same sentence as the name Peter means 'rock'. But what should we conclude from this?

Some traditions, mainly Catholic and Orthodox, assert this is *all* about Peter. He *was* the rock on which Jesus would build. In contrast, Protestant and evangelical movements, perhaps wishing to distance themselves from Catholic doctrine, maintain that in the second part of what Jesus said the focus then shifts away from the man to the revelation he had just experienced. This, the divine revelation, was the rock Jesus was talking about, and it is on such a recognition of who Jesus is and a consequent statement of faith that the true church of Christ would be built.

Certainly faith in Jesus as Messiah and Son of God is essential, but it is also reasonable to believe that Peter, after this divinely inspired confession, was being personally highlighted by Jesus. As a main apostle and leader, he would be a dominant part of the rock on which Jesus was promising to build his church. This can be so without extending to him the role of Pope or Bishop of Rome!

It is also quite well known that in the gospel text Jesus is recorded as saying, 'You are *Petros*, and on this *petra* I will build my church.' Although these are Greek words, research has suggested that both words may have entered the Hebrew language as loanwords, which are words that transfer to another language while remaining in their original form. For instance, many examples exist between French and English. We easily use 'bourgeois', 'souvenir', 'etiquette' and many more, as well as phrases such as 'déjà vu' and 'avant-garde'. The French have taken 'le weekend' and 'le parking' into their language, as well as phrases such as 'happy hour'!

A similar relationship between Greek and Hebrew is perhaps more difficult to ascertain and is beyond the scope of this book, but it is interesting to note that the Greek *Petros* was already, or would soon become, used in the names of Hebrew people and places. So Jesus may have used these actual words in his pun, or something similar may have been at work in the Hebrew he spoke.

However, more important for our purposes is to understand the difference between the two related words for rock. *Petra* is bedrock or a massive rock formation; *petros* is a smaller piece of rock, an unattached stone or, at most, a boulder. This should inform our view of what Jesus was saying about Peter and his role. Basically, he would be a little bit of something much bigger.

If Jesus had said, 'You are Peter, and on *you* I will build my church', then it would have been clearer. But 'on *this* rock' creates ambiguity. If only we had been there we may have been able to resolve this uncertainty. For instance, we might have noticed where Jesus was looking when he said '*this*'. Or perhaps where he was pointing.

A rabbi often illustrated his teaching from what his disciples could see around them. He may have pointed to something at the same time as speaking. He also deliberately took them to places where his teaching would be reinforced by what was there. So, was there any rock near where Jesus said these words?

The location Jesus chose for this time with his disciples is described as being in the region of Caesarea Philippi in the northernmost part of the land, near the ancient city of Dan. This was a pagan stronghold dedicated to the god Pan, with a temple and caves in a massive wall of rock over 30 metres high and 150 metres wide. The city of Caesarea Philippi was built on the top of this cliff face. In addition, the caves there were regarded as an entrance to the underworld and were referred to as 'the gates of Hades'.

The whole area provided a graphic representation of what Jesus was proclaiming. This was not a coincidence. Jesus could point to the geographical features around him to reinforce his message. Of course, he did not plan to build a physical church there, but the spiritual counterpart was clear. We can imagine him looking first at Petros, then up at the *'petra'*, and perhaps back to Petros. What Jesus would build would be stronger than anything here, and Peter would have a major part to play in this. Would he be solid enough to withstand the pressures? Would he be strong enough for the spiritual battle? After the revelation Peter received, Jesus believed so, enough to give him a new name to reflect what would be required of him.

But there is a further point to be made. Jesus was not just engaging in amusing wordplay. He would have used the word 'rock' to plant a further seed in Peter's mind. A rabbi would often drop hints from the scriptures, which his disciples would be expected to pick up. Just one word would be enough for them to make a connection and draw an extra message. Here 'rock' would remind them of Isaiah 51:1-2, 'Look to the rock from which you were cut and to the quarry from which you were hewn; look to Abraham, your father, and to Sarah, who gave you birth.' Peter would have been thrilled with this! 'Jesus is comparing me to Abraham, the father of many nations! He is saying I can be a rock for him, just like Abraham was for God at the beginning of our history!'

There is a later rabbinic *midrash* (a Jewish commentary upon a biblical text) which is worth quoting. It also portrays Abraham as 'rock' and shows how the Hebraic mind works by trying to understand God through stories. Here, God is wanting to create the world but wondering if it will be worth it given all the wickedness that he foresees will result. In typical Jewish fashion, God's dilemma is compared to a king who desired to build a palace. The story continues:

> 'He began digging, searching for solid rock on which he could lay foundations but he found only mire. He dug in several other sites, always with the same results. However, the king did not give up. He dug in still another location. This time he struck solid rock. "Here", he said, "I will build", and he laid foundations and built. In the same manner, the Holy One, before he created the world, sat and examined the generations of Enosh and the generation of the Flood. "How can I create the world when those wicked people will appear and provoke me to anger?" he said. When, however, the Holy One saw Abraham, he said, "Here I have found solid rock on which I can build and upon which I can lay the world's foundations."' (Yalkut Shimoni, on Num. 23:9)

When God looked further down the line and saw Abraham, he knew he should go ahead! Here was someone he could partner with to put things right. Is this how Jesus now saw Peter?

Jesus continued to build up Peter's confidence with another image full of biblical references and allusions. Peter would be given the keys of the kingdom of heaven (not of any gates, pearly or otherwise!). What would Peter make of this?

Keys are symbolic of trust. Those who hold them are regarded as responsible and reliable. Again Jesus dropped a particular word into the conversation to guide Peter's thinking. On hearing Jesus mention keys, Peter may well have thought of two Old Testament passages full of meaning.

In Isaiah 22:20-22 we read about a faithful steward called Eliakim who was a palace administrator under King Hezekiah. He was chosen to replace another palace official of high position, Shebna, who was in disgrace for taking advantage of his privileged status. Through a sense of his own self-importance Shebna wanted to be buried in the palace and so had arranged for a conspicuous monumental rock-tomb to be hewn there (Isa. 22:15-19). As a result he was ousted and the more humble and worthy Eliakim was given the key of the house of David instead. The statement in Isaiah 20:22 is particularly memorable, and one that Jesus later used of himself: 'These are the words of him who is holy and true, who holds the key of David. What he opens no-one can shut and what he shuts no-one can open' (Rev. 3:7).

In another passage, 1 Chronicles 9:22-27, we learn about the four principal gatekeepers of the Temple and the trust placed in them as key holders. Their special responsibility for the rooms and treasuries meant they spent the night at their stations as they had charge of the key for opening the house of God each morning.

This contrasts with a rabbinic story concerning the destruction of the first Temple. Those in charge of the keys acknowledged they had failed in their duty and confessed to God, 'Since we have failed at being faithful stewards, let these keys be given back to you.' As they threw them up towards heaven, a large hand received them!

A similar anecdote is recorded in a Jewish pseudepigraphical text of the early second century AD. Regarding the second Temple, 2 Baruch 10:18 states, 'You priests, take the keys of the sanctuary and throw them up to heaven above and give them to the Lord and say, "Guard your house yourself, for we have been found to be false stewards."'

The point of both of these stories is that God is the true owner of such keys, and only gives them to those he considers faithful and trustworthy. In our passage, Jesus declared that Peter merited similar recognition in the church Jesus would build. But what might this mean in practice? For this we need a correct interpretation of another Hebraic idiom: binding and loosing.

These two words, bind and loose, are frequently taken out of the context of Matthew 16:19 and misapplied. The translations are correct, but their specific use within the Jewish world of the time is often ignored.

To use them in the context of spiritual warfare is at best misguided and at worst potentially dangerous. Although the word 'bind' is used elsewhere in an analogy by Jesus about tying up a strong man before robbing him (Matt. 12:29), when taken as part of a pair with 'loose' it has nothing to do with binding demons. After all, would we want anyone to loose demons as part of their ministry?!

The correct usage of this idiomatic phrase is found within rabbinic literature. Teachers of the Law were constantly required to make rulings when interpreting scriptural commands. For instance, when it came to the Sabbath and work, what exactly was permitted and forbidden? These decisions were then expressed in terms of binding and loosing. To bind was to forbid; to loose was to permit.

Today we might say, 'I bind you from walking on the grass', or 'I loose you to make a copy of my picture'. But we don't! It is not part of our language. But that was what Peter would have understood.

He had just received a new name, indicating a new start which would need a new resolve. And he had been promised the 'keys of heaven', reflecting trust in his position of authority. Part of this mandate was the responsibility to make decisions in the church which Jesus would be building. Would Peter get them right? What a burden that could be!

So Jesus provided Peter with more reassurance by saying that what he decided would have heaven's backing. His decisions would be upheld by God. This is not saying that God would automatically agree with Peter! Rather that Peter would get it right because 'heaven was looking on' and

God was guiding those decisions. This is reflected in the alternative, and probably more accurate, translation of 'will have been' bound or loosed in heaven, usually placed in a footnote.

The church would be a new phenomenon and would face situations unlike any before. New decisions would have to be made. Even what Peter knew from his existing scriptures may not suffice. But by hearing Jesus talk in this way, taking something familiar from his Jewish background, he could rest assured that he would be able to cope. In such new and demanding circumstances, fear and worry can easily lead to a paralysis of indecision or a rush into wrong decisions. Jesus was effectively saying, 'Fear not! Peter, you *will* get it right. Even though I won't be around, I'll make sure of that!'

This whole episode was a life-defining moment for Peter. A name change in the Bible was always significant. How often now do we think of him as Simon bar Jonah? We even refer to him as Peter when discussing events in his life before this moment when his name was changed.

We have previously looked at John chapter 21 when thinking about Peter's betrayal and what this might mean in terms of his discipleship. It is interesting to note here that before Jesus restored Peter to discipleship he referred to him as 'Simon, son of John' (John 21:15, 16, 17). This can pass by unnoticed to a casual reader, but Jesus deliberately used Peter's old name three times to make a point. Peter would have been stirred by the memory of the last time Jesus referred to him this way, here in Matthew 16:17, and how far he had fallen from this glorious moment of revelation and approval. Peter's temporary loss of discipleship was reflected in how Jesus addressed him at this point, but it was not to be long before he was 'the rock' again. What's in a name? A lot, it seems, when it's Peter.

To sum up, Peter would be solid as a rock and a founding part of something much bigger than he could have imagined. He would reliably be able to lock and unlock situations that otherwise would have been beyond his understanding. And he would make complex decisions that were guaranteed to be in line with God's will.

Peter may not have understood all the future implications of what Jesus had said, but at least he had understood the words. Hopefully, now that we have listened carefully to the Jewish Jesus, we do too.

But what about the other disciples who had been listening in? Did they feel left out? Resentful? And did this 'binding and loosing' actually happen in practice? We follow this up in our next chapter.

Chapter Seven

Two or Three?

Matthew 18:15-20

We ended the last chapter by wondering how the other disciples might have been impacted by what Jesus said to Peter in Matthew 16:17-19. Did they feel left out? Would this include them in any way? Well, they didn't have long to find out. Just a couple of chapters, in fact!

Matthew chapter 18 is the fourth of the five teaching sections in Matthew's Gospel, and one of the training sessions for the disciples. It is in the middle of this chapter that we find Jesus repeating to all his disciples what he had said to Peter about binding and loosing (v. 8). If you recall, this expression relates to decision making in which to bind was to forbid something and to loose was to allow something. This was how rabbis declared rulings on questions based upon the Law and its practices, and Peter had already been told by Jesus that he would be required to make similar judgements within the context of the new community of believers that Jesus would establish, what today we call the church. Now, in Matthew 18:18, we learn that this would apply to all the apostles. Any of them could be called upon to interpret Scripture, settle disputes and find answers in time of crisis.

We also asked last time how this 'binding' and 'loosing' might work out in practice, so before we study our passage in Matthew, we will consider some incidents in Acts where this kind of leadership could be said to have taken place.

In Acts 5:1-11, we have the dramatic account of the deaths of Ananias and his wife Sapphira due to deceit over their finances. Peter knew Ananias was lying over the amount of money he was bringing as an offering to the church community following the sale of a piece of land. However, when he challenged him over this, Peter may well have been startled at the outcome when Ananias fell down dead in front of him! But three hours later, when Sapphira also 'came in, not knowing what had happened' (v. 7), Peter was prepared. God had acted and, when Sapphira repeated the same lie, Peter was confident to make his ruling – 'they will carry you out also' (v. 9). Which, of course, they did. Was this a case of Peter carrying out the sort of judicial ruling implied by what Jesus had said about 'binding' and 'loosing'? Certainly heaven backed up what Peter had declared!

In Acts 6:1-6, we see another important decision being made, this time regarding the need to support certain widows. Some of them were being overlooked in favour of others when it came to the daily distribution of food. This had to be put right but not at the expense of deflecting the apostles away from the ministry of prayer and the teaching of the word of God. So a decision was made to appoint seven others to the responsibility of ensuring these widows were adequately cared for. To be fair, this may not seem such a clear case of 'binding' and 'loosing', and so far our two examples from Acts may seem relatively minor compared to what was about to unfold.

In Acts 15, a major council was held in Jerusalem to resolve an unexpected crisis – Gentiles were becoming believers in the Jewish Messiah, and receiving the same Holy Spirit! How should they be received into the church? Should they be accepted without first circumcising them and commanding them to keep the Law of Moses? Here was a raging controversy which threatened to split the church at an early stage. The process of settling it was a fascinating one!

Various cases were made, which the apostles and elders considered. Then Peter stood up and 'loosed', or released, Gentiles from any requirement to keep the Law of Moses (vv. 7-11). James agreed, and he also 'loosed' them (v. 19). But he also 'bound' them by making certain prohibitions concerning food that had been offered to idols, sexual immorality, the meat of strangled animals and blood (v. 20). The latter refers to meat from which the blood had not been removed at the time of death as the animals had been strangled rather than bled to death.

The full reasoning behind these particular 'bindings' is beyond our discussion here, but we should note this 'binding and loosing' was then written down, making it official. It could then be sent to the new Gentile believers as something to be universally known and upheld.

A tricky and potentially damaging crisis had been averted. Peter and the others must have been thankful that Jesus had prepared them so thoroughly, and to know that 'heaven was in agreement' with their decision. It should be added that in all these matters 'heaven' is always an alternative way of saying 'God', especially in Matthew's Gospel with its sensitivity towards Jewish readers who preferred not to use God's name. There is no sense that

81

anyone other than God the Father is involved. This is not the outcome of a debate in a heavenly court.

We now return to our passage in Matthew chapter 18 in which the 'binding and loosing' statement is contained within a section (v. 15-20) that deserves our full consideration as this provides the context not only to verse 18 but to all of the statements made within these verses.

It is not always noticed that this passage concerns church discipline, or as the New International Version heads it, 'Dealing with sin in the church'. When a brother sins, what should be the response? Is there a correct procedure for dealing with such demanding pastoral situations? In particular, what kind of rulings would be endorsed by heaven? In answer to these important but difficult questions, Jesus provides a three-stage process of increasing severity and consequences. It is then that we get the promise that whatever the apostles 'bind' or 'loose' will be sanctioned by heaven. It is regrettable that verse 18 is often detached from what has gone before and so its true message is lost, usually to be replaced by something wide of the mark, such as spiritual warfare or dealing with demons.

It should now be clear that a correct understanding of verse 18 depends upon verses 15 to 17, but what about the following two verses, 19 and 20? Are these also attached to the preceding verses or do they stand alone? Once more, if only we had been there it might have been obvious what Jesus intended! But perhaps we can deduce the answer from the text itself.

Both of these verses are often quoted out of context as though individually they can be applied to any situation we want. In particular, verse 20 is a favourite when the attendance at a prayer meeting is rather thin! Never mind, at least Jesus is here!

Some do advocate a more general application of verses 19 to 20, separate from the immediate context of verses 15 to 18. They point to the opening word 'again' which they suggest indicates a fresh start rather than a continuation. They also argue that the use of the word 'anything' or 'whatever' in verse 19 opens up a wider scope of things that may be asked for, rather than just what is needed in the process of dealing with a wayward brother or sister.

However, others say that a section as small as verses 19 to 20 is more likely to be attached to other verses nearby than stand completely alone, and in this case there is a convincing argument for the unity of all of verses 15 to 20. This is based upon the phrase 'two or three' found in verse 20, which refers back to the number of witnesses needed in verse 16 where the 'one or two others' plus yourself creates the necessary 'two or three'. This is in accordance with the general requirement of Deuteronomy 19:15, 'A matter must be established by the testimony of two or three witnesses.' On this basis alone, verses 15 to 20 must constitute a unified section of teaching from Jesus and it is wrong to pluck certain verses out of this context for other purposes.

Furthermore, there is the wider context of the rest of chapter 18. In verse 21 Peter asks about forgiving his brother when he sins against him. This will be discussed as part of our next chapter, but for now we simply note that Peter is picking up here on Jesus' teaching which has flowed from verse 15 onwards: 'If a brother or sister sins . . .'

Overall, then, the context suggests the matter to be agreed upon in verse 19 relates to the discipline of unrepentant brothers. The two or three who are to arbitrate in the issue should come together in the name of Jesus, knowing they can ask him for whatever they need to reach the right decision, and be reassured that the judgement given (the 'binding' or 'loosing'), whether against the brother or in his favour, will be according to God's will.

How discipline is done, and is seen to be done, can be as important as the outcome. This is Jesus' aim in what he is teaching here. He knows there is a huge responsibility involved in dealing with matters of discipline, forgiveness and restoration, the consequences of which can be far-reaching and ruinous. Those making such decisions could feel overwhelmed. 'What if we don't get this right?' What we read here is intended to give them, and the rest of the church, confidence in the process that Jesus has outlined.

Even when all this has been explained, you will still hear verse 19 or verse 20 being quoted out of context by many well-meaning Christians. Is this totally wrong or is there an excuse for them? Of course, Jesus is with us in prayer meetings, Bible study and the like, but this is usually through the Spirit. However, the more personal 'I am with them' mentioned at the end of this passage is intended for situations involving serious escalations of sin between believers.

It is worth pointing out, though, that in Jewish circles an extension to a teaching is sometimes allowed. This is called making a *midrash* and is a way of authorising an application that is not explicit in the text itself but which is in line with it. So perhaps in this case, allowances can be made!

The trouble with having a lesser interpretation applied outside the clear context is that it can become the norm while the original meaning is lost or ignored. This is what tends to happen here with these two verses. But then, realising what is actually meant in these verses might also cause problems. We would then have to practise church discipline in the way Jesus instructs! And that is not something that most churches want to engage in or even think about.

Two other points are worth mentioning. Some say these verses reflect the idea of a *minyan*, the quorum of ten men over the age of thirteen required for Jewish worship or prayer. Here, though, it is not ten as in a synagogue, but two or three, plus Jesus himself. Moreover, in the Mishnah (the collection of Jewish writings mentioned in an earlier chapter), we read in one place that 'Whenever ten are gathered for prayer, there the Shekinah rests' (Sanhedrin 39) and in another, 'When three sit as judges, the Shekinah is with them' (Berachot 6). The Shekinah is the manifest presence of God.

Certainly the similarities with Jesus' teaching are striking, as is also the case in another part of the Mishnah which contains statements such as 'if two sit together and words of the Law are spoken between them, the Divine Presence rests between them' and 'if three have eaten at one table and have spoken over it words of the Law, it is as if they had eaten from the table of God' (Pirke Aboth, 3:2, 3).

Finally, we need to address another issue that arises in this passage and that of our previous chapter (Matt. 16:17-19). With all the debate about rock, confession, keys, binding and loosing, the real point is often missed. In these two passages, and *only in these two*, does Jesus use the word 'church'. Nowhere else in any of the gospels does this word occur. And that leads to a curious incident.

With apologies to Conan Doyle, I would like to comment on 'the curious incident of the disciples in the daytime'. But the disciples did nothing in the daytime! And that was the curious incident. Jesus seems to mention something totally new, using a strange word that they had never heard before, and they remain silent. There should have been a reaction. Either they would have muttered to themselves, 'What does he mean by "church"?', or we would read that later they came to Jesus privately, saying, 'Rabbi, tell us more about this new idea you've got called "church".'

The explanation for this absence of comment is quite simple. The disciples weren't at all surprised by what Jesus said because he didn't say 'church'! The word is not a translation of either the Greek in the text or anything Jesus would have said in Hebrew. Rather, it was implanted into our English translations at the time of King James and the Authorised Version to support the Church of England of which the King was head – that's King James, not King Jesus! And this word has remained in most of our Bibles ever since.

Earlier translations, for instance Tyndale's, used a different word, such as 'assembly' or 'gathering'. The King James Version drew heavily upon Tyndale and is largely the same but with several key exceptions, the main ones being all the ecclesiastical words that were imposed into the translation by edict of the king ('church' was number 3 of 15 such edicts). The whole matter was politically motivated, and the word 'church' should not appear in our Bibles at all, including the rest of the New Testament.

Why does this matter? Isn't this just a translational nicety? Far from it. This is not a mere quibble over vocabulary. The consequences can be far-reaching and profound. It means we look at what we call 'church' today and assume Jesus must have meant this because that's what we read he said. But most churches today are not run along the lines Jesus envisaged or are anything like those that existed in the first century, which may explain why certain Biblical principles, including discipline, are not in place at all.

Man has built something quite different from what Jesus intended in these two passages in Matthew and which he started to build with Peter, Paul and the other apostles. What we see around us today is largely the work of our hands, rather than what Jesus promised. We have many institutional churches and occasional one-man shows, but rarely the Spirit-led gifted assemblies or communities in which all members operate as a body under the 'head builder', King Jesus.

So what did Jesus say? Most likely the Hebrew word would have been *qahal*, meaning 'community', 'assembly' or 'congregation'. This is a word the disciples would have recognised and understood as it was a description of Israel after God had rescued them out of Egypt and called them to be a new nation under him. Repeatedly in the Old Testament we read that Israel gathered or assembled before God and as a whole were referred to as a community (see, for example, Exod. 35:1, Lev. 4:13-14, Deut. 5:22).

This word, *qahal*, not only describes Israel then but also carries through into what Jesus was going to do when he announced to his disciples, 'I will build my community, and I'm starting with you.' The equivalent Greek word to the Hebrew *qahal* is *ekklesia*, which occurs over a hundred times in the New Testament, including throughout Paul's letters and the book of Revelation. But here *ekklesia* is always mistranslated as 'church', rather than being given its proper meaning of 'assembly' or 'community'. The only exceptions are in Acts 19 where it is used in a non-religious sense to designate a legal assembly or riotous mob (v. 32, 39, 41).

Others have said, and written, much more on the true meaning of 'church', which interested readers can follow up. Here we have had to be brief. Meanwhile, in our next chapter we will look at the rest of Matthew chapter 18 as Peter picks up the theme of brothers who fall short and need forgiveness.

Chapter Eight

All the Sevens, Seventy-Seven

Matthew 18:21-35

In this chapter we will be focusing on Matthew 18:21-35, which we observed last time follows on naturally from the preceding section (v. 15-20). This is seen not just through the common theme of sin and repentance, but also by virtue of the common words about a brother who sins against another (v. 15, 21). The difference in verses 21-35 is that Peter asks a supplementary question about forgiveness.

But before we consider his question we must clear up an initial point. To whom is Peter referring? Who is this potential wrongdoer? A translation may have *'someone who sins'*, in an attempt to be gender inclusive and avoid the rather clunky 'brother or sister' which can be irksome on repeated use. However, the Greek remains *adelphos*, which refers to a fellow disciple of either gender, so we will continue to use brother while acknowledging that sinfulness is not a male preserve and the female of the species is equally likely to be 'the one who sins'.

Incidentally, the passage ends in verse 35 with another mention of 'brother' (or sister) so forming what is known as an *inclusio*, a literary device to indicate the boundaries of a section, the top and tail of a passage, so that we know that this has now come to a conclusion.

However we choose to translate *adelphos* it is best to regard Peter's question as still referring to the new community that Jesus will build. The word 'someone' might suggest it could be anyone at all, but the context remains those believers we regard as our brothers and sisters. There will be enough sins to deal with here!

Let's get back to the question itself and notice that Peter makes an attempt to answer it himself. 'How many times should I forgive my brother? How about up to seven? What's your response to that, Rabbi?'

Peter's suggestion makes sense in several ways. Rather than placing a numerical limit on forgiveness, Peter may have been using the number seven in its idiomatic or symbolic meaning of fullness or completion. It is also worth noting that this question was a typical one asked of rabbis generally. This is something any disciple would want to know of the one they were following, so that they could do the same. The answer given would indicate whether their rabbi was of the strict or lenient school of interpretation. Seven may have been a standard answer, especially by those who tended to encourage mercy and forgiveness. Perhaps Peter was second-guessing here on the basis of what he knew of his rabbi so far.

This would be a more convincing idea if Jesus had already taught Luke 17:3-4! It may not be easy to ascertain which passage came first, or even if they are parallel passages, but in Luke's shorter version Jesus advocates forgiving the same brother seven times per day! Again this might be symbolic rather than numerical. Be fulsome in your forgiveness! Nevertheless, this does seem to be very generous and potentially open to abuse. Is the repentance genuine every time? It is possibly for this reason that certain Jewish traditions suggested three times was adequate. It was unwise to go on forgiving endlessly, for if someone did not change their behaviour after the first few times, then they never would.

The Mishnah (that collection of Jewish writings we keep referring to) has a section on the Day of Atonement called Yoma. Here we read that 'If a man said, "I will sin and repent, and sin again and repent", he will be given no chance to repent. If he said, "I will sin and the Day of Atonement will effect atonement", then the Day of Atonement effects no atonement' (Yoma 8:9). It adds that if the transgression is between man and God then the Day of Atonement effects atonement, but if the transgression is between man and his fellow, then the Day of Atonement effects atonement only if he has appeased his fellow.

It would seem from this that repentance has to be taken seriously and known to be genuine if forgiveness is to be offered and atonement made. Discernment is needed in this important matter. In addition, some evidence of reconciliation is needed if it is a case of brother sinning against brother.

It is worth pursuing this just a little further. The Talmud, which is a collection of commentaries on the Mishnah, includes an interesting reflection on Yoma 8:9. 'When a person commits a transgression the first time, he is forgiven; a second time, he is forgiven; a third time, he is forgiven; but the fourth time, he is not forgiven.'

The purpose behind this comment is to prevent us thinking that God forgives too easily, and the rationale is based upon two scriptures. 'God does all these things to a man – twice, even three times – to turn back his soul from the pit, that the light of life may shine on him' (Job 33:29-30). The implication is that after three times he is not to be forgiven. This is backed up by another text: 'For three transgressions of Israel, but for four I will not turn back my wrath' (Amos 2:6).

This might seem a rather obscure, even dubious, way of applying scripture, but that is how the ancient Jewish mind worked. After all this, we might think that listening to Jesus is easy! So let's return to Matthew chapter 18 and see if this is the case!

So how many times should we forgive our brother? Tradition said three. Peter raises this to seven, perhaps expecting Jesus to exceed other rabbis and agree with the idea of fullness and completion. But Jesus replies in a way that may seem surprising to us, though not to Peter. This is because Jesus is dropping a hint from the Hebrew scriptures that Peter would be well aware of. But are we?

Jesus comes up with the rather unusual number of seventy-seven. Is this just some random multiple of seven? Or a higher use of 'sevens'? Some translations suggest in a footnote the possibility of the number really being seventy *times* seven as it is possible to interpret the Greek phrase that way round, as opposed to seventy-seven *times*. Should we prefer this alternative? After all, four hundred and ninety is a much bigger number and surely Jesus is telling us to stretch our ability to forgive to the utmost!

But to assume this means we would miss the clue that Jesus is giving us. Here Jesus is reminding Peter of another place in the Bible where the number seventy-seven has a significant and related use. In Genesis 4:24, Lamech boasts to his wives about his ability to extract revenge. 'If Cain is avenged seven times, then Lamech seventy-seven times.' This was not just well known from scripture; the phrase 'the revenge of Lamech' had gone into common usage to express the desire for reprisal and retribution far in excess of anyone else or what could reasonably be tolerated.

What we need to understand is that here Jesus is replying to Peter with a *remez*, a Hebrew word which means hint, clue or allusion. This was a common rabbinic teaching device of the time which we will come across many more times in this book. In a *remez*, a word (or in this case, a number) was deliberately chosen and used in order to link back to a part of scripture that would illustrate the rabbi's message and even take it further in the mind of the listener. We have already seen this at work in a previous chapter when Jesus used the words 'rock' and 'keys' to make Peter more aware of his new role.

Jesus often used a *remez* in his teaching, as we shall see throughout this book, but he wouldn't suddenly announce, 'Here's another *remez* for you!' For a start, the method didn't receive this name until much later, in the medieval period. But there was no need to send out such an alert. The disciples would be listening out for such links and, because they had memorised their scriptures from an early age, their minds would be attuned to receiving the hint.

But what if they missed it? Would the rabbi then give them the reference or open up the scroll for them and show them? Not at all! That was not only impossible but undesirable. It was not a rabbi's task to spell everything out. Instead his role was to set up journeys of discovery in which the disciples had to uncover certain truths for themselves. This was how they grew. If they missed it, their loss!

How would we fare with this process? We would have to admit we might struggle. But we might manage better with New Testament verses. Just two words might suffice: 'For God . . .' Need I go on? 'For God so . . .' Do you have it yet? 'For God so loved . . .' Now you've got there! You're away! But how far? Just a single verse, the famous John 3:16? What about verse 17, or the whole of chapter 3? The idea behind the method of *remez* is not to create sound bites but to reference large passages. The initial 'starter' should add new levels of meaning to the rabbi's teaching by triggering off whole swathes of Scripture.

Meanwhile, back in Matthew, we should now understand that here Jesus is not providing a numerical value to aim for. This is not a counting exercise, a set of boxes to tick off, or a limit to strive towards. Rather, it serves to direct our attention to the revenge of Lamech, which was greater than the seven of Cain. So Jesus picks up the number seven that Peter offers and answers his question in an indirect but potent manner.

The *remez* to Lamech sets up a contrast. Are we as willing and eager to forgive as Lamech was to take vengeance? For him, forgiveness was non-existent. Revenge was the only thing on his mind, constantly, whatever the offence. Jesus is telling us to be equally extravagant in forgiveness, going far beyond any wrong done to us. We are to be Lamech's polar opposite, and with forgiveness 'outnumber' evil, even in all its extremes and excesses.

To follow this up, Jesus now tells a story, one which also focuses on extremes and excesses. We shall look at several parables in later chapters, but for now we simply note that Jesus did not invent the parable. Typically he took up something already familiar in the Jewish world and made it an integral part of his teaching strategy.

Parables were designed to both illuminate and challenge, and often contained at least one shock and one twist. In the parable in Matthew 18:23-35 it is not long before we meet our first shock – someone owes ten thousand talents! This is a huge amount of money. According to one calculation it was about the equivalent today of three lifetimes of earnings! What kind of king allows that amount of debt to build up?

Is Jesus offering another *remez* here? The same amount occurs in Esther 3:9, where ten thousand talents of silver (340 tons!) is the payment Haman arranges with Xerxes for the purposes of destroying the Jewish people. In this case a connection may be hard to find so perhaps it is a coincidence. Not every similarity has to be a *remez*!

Either way, such an amount could never be repaid even if everything the man had, including wife and children, was sold. So why does the king order this to happen? Here is another surprise! This is not a solution. In fact it sounds more like a Lamech-style revenge, with the whole family being punished too! What do we now make of the king?

The servant's plea for more time is still not a solution, and eventually the king shows pity and cancels the debt.

But the tragedy of the story, and its main point, is that the servant leaves the presence of a compassionate king free from debt but unchanged in his attitude towards his fellow men. When a second servant appears, who owes a much smaller amount (perhaps just a few weeks' wages), a similar scene is played out (verse 29 is almost identical to verse 26), but with a different result, and another shock then ensues. On refusing his fellow servant the same forgiveness he himself has just received, the first servant seemingly has his huge debt restored and ends up in the same prison into which he had thrown the second servant. There he will be tortured forever, or at least for the rest of his life, as we already know that he can never repay that original debt.

The main point is clear. We have been forgiven much and this should be reflected in our attitude towards others. Nobody can sin against us as much as we have against God, and this must be our guide towards extravagant forgiveness. Remember, Jesus is still replying to Peter's question and reinforcing the message of the 'seventy-seven'.

But this might still leave us with some disturbing questions about the story. If the king represents our heavenly Father, then why does he react like Lamech, piling on the extra vengeance? Can God really reverse his decision to forgive us completely? Does one moment of unforgiveness result in eternal torture? Is there now no way out at all for the unmerciful servant?

The point is, tempting though it is to draw lots of direct comparisons, parables are not parallels where every bit has to equate. For instance, in another parable on prayer, God seems to be likened to an unjust judge who doesn't care about men or fear God (Luke 18:1-8)! But the parable is about persistent prayer, not the nature of God. In Matthew chapter 18, the focus is on the unnamed servant (that could be you again!) and his attitude. The rest of the story is circumstantial, set up to provide that focal point. That is how parables usually work. It is also worth knowing, for instance, that selling off all a debtor's goods and family was actually a common custom of the time, so it fits the story well, without reflecting on the character of the king.

But there is also an interesting alternative way of looking at the ending (v. 34). Some say there is an ambiguity over the pronouns and that the final 'he' is the second servant, not the first. In addition, it is thought that the Greek verb *apodo*, translated 'pay back', can also mean 'cancel', 'release' or 'forgive'. So the final part of the parable could be read as, 'until he (the first servant) should cancel all that he (the second servant) owed (him, the first servant)'.

In fact, Greek texts suggest 'pay all that was *due to him*' as a direct translation, which seems to go some way towards this alternative ending. This now makes the debt the smaller one, which is reasonable as this *is* payable. However, the verb is still 'pay' rather than 'cancel', so whether the Greek text can really support all this is something that scholars must decide. But it does change how the story plays out. The servant can still never pay back his huge debt to the king, but the opportunity remains for him to forgive his fellow servant the small debt owed to him. He won't be released unless he does this, but once he does, then the door will open out of this prison of his own making.

In this scenario, the parable is more about life now rather than eternal torment in the hereafter, as is so often taught. Moreover, the story is left hanging, waiting for us to finish it, which, as we have seen before, is often the case with the teaching of Jesus. So could this be what the Jewish Jesus actually said in his own language? Is this what we would have heard if listening to him at the time? Over to you to decide!

We will return to parables shortly. Meanwhile, as promised earlier, we will next revisit the first time Jesus 'opened his mouth and spoke': that famous discourse on a Galilean hillside where the massed crowds heard with amazement a rabbi speak with an authority unlike any other.

PART TWO

Sermons and Stories

Chapter Nine

The Law is an Asset

Matthew 5:17-20

In this chapter we return to the early teaching of Jesus as recorded by Matthew in what we call the Sermon on the Mount. We have already set the scene for this in a previous chapter, when we said we would find in this sermon plenty of examples of Jesus teaching in a Jewish rabbinic manner. In this chapter and the next three we will look in detail at some of these.

We start with a short but vital passage on one of the most misunderstood aspects of Judaism, and therefore of the roots of the Christian faith, namely the Law. Matthew 5:17-20 is full of Hebraic words and expressions, and highlights the absolute necessity of listening carefully to what the Jewish Jesus actually said, not what we think he said.

Before we come to the main points, an initial observation is worth making from these verses. Whenever Jesus uses the phrase 'I have come' or 'not come' (for instance, v. 17), he is not referring to his incarnation, or to a visit to Galilee or any other location. Rather this is a Hebraic way of declaring intent. Here is a task to be undertaken not a journey that has been made. Effectively, Jesus is stating one of his mission aims.

In particular, in verse 17, Jesus wants his listeners to be clear about what his mission does *not* entail. So he tells them first of all what *not* to think about his intention. It is always good to clear up any confusion first, so let us do the same before we investigate his message.

In Hebraic terms, when it comes to the Law 'abolish' and 'fulfil' have different meanings from the way we might use them in our culture today. It is often thought that when Jesus said he would fulfil the Law, it meant he would keep every bit of it perfectly. However, this was not possible, not even for Jesus. Although we believe Jesus lived a blameless life in every way, he could not have kept all of the six hundred and thirteen commandments. That may come as a surprise, until you realise that some of the laws could only be kept by women, those concerning menstruation for instance (Lev. 15:19-33)! There are also certain laws that are for men only, so no human could keep all the Law anyway, however much he or she tried! Moreover, some of the laws were only for the priests, so these wouldn't apply to Jesus either. Overall, we need to be clear that the word 'fulfil' does not refer to whether laws are kept or broken.

Nor does 'fulfil' mean making up for anything that is lacking in the Law, or bringing it to completion in any way. Jesus did not come to make the Law perfect; according to Psalm 19:7, it was already perfect. Moreover, Paul declares the Law is also holy, righteous, good and spiritual (Rom. 7:12, 14). So what could possibly be lacking?

Equally, 'abolishing' the Law did not mean annulling it or setting it aside. Why do this anyway, when the psalmist declared it to be a delight and a joy (Ps. 1:2, 119:92, 174)? Overall, to the Jewish way of thinking, the Law was an asset.

So what is Jesus referring to here in Matthew 5:17? The answer once again depends upon a Hebraic perspective. In this case, the context is that of rabbinic debate about interpreting the Law correctly. Within this setting, these two words are Hebraisms with their own specific meanings: to 'abolish' means to misinterpret; to 'fulfil' means to interpret correctly.

Within arguments over interpretation of the Law a typical accusation would be 'You are abolishing the Law', meaning you are undermining it by giving a wrong interpretation. No-one can actually abolish or destroy God's Law as such, but you can render a particular law ineffective if you say it means something other than, or less than, it really does. If people don't know how to keep a law properly then this is equivalent to destroying or annulling it. Similarly, to fulfil a law is to explain it correctly so that it can be kept as intended.

To summarise what Jesus is saying here, the following paraphrase may be useful: 'Do not imagine for one moment that I intend to weaken or negate the Law by my interpretations. My purpose is to establish it more firmly. By correctly interpreting it, I will set it on a stronger footing and make it even more lasting.'

At this point we should explain what 'Law' means to the Jewish mind, which again differs from the way we usually understand the word. We tend to think of a legal system in which the Law is something to be avoided. Break it and get caught, and unwelcome consequences may follow.

But the Hebrew word *Torah* conveys something totally different. Its root meaning is guidance, instruction or teaching, and derives from a word that conveys the giving of direction. The intention of the Law is to guide us towards a target so that we might hit the mark rather than fall short. Missing the mark, or falling short, were expressions for sin in both Judaism and early Christianity (see Rom. 3:23).

Moreover, Torah was much more than just a collection of laws, a list of 'thou shalts' and 'thou shalt nots'. The word 'Law' makes us think of Moses and the first five books of the Old Testament, but we forget that most of this is narrative. These stories are also meant to guide and teach us. The idea of Torah includes these too and can even be extended to other parts of the scriptures if these teach us the will of God. Any narrative can be useful in showing us the right way to live, illustrating the consequences of our actions, whether right or wrong.

It is also crucial to realise that the Law was not given to the Jewish people so they could earn or merit any kind of salvation. Keeping the Law was not about getting into God's good books or winning his favour. God liberated or 'saved' his people first when he brought them out of Egypt. They had done nothing to deserve this. He did it because he loved them and was in a covenant relationship with them through Abraham. Then he gave them the Law as part of another covenant (with Moses) so that they might show gratitude for his redemption and learn to live in line with his will as his chosen people.

When we realise what Torah means and how it featured in the history of the Jewish people, then we see that God is not primarily a lawgiver, but a loving father who wants to instruct his children and guide them into the best possible life. We can also understand why Jesus had a high esteem for the Law and so wanted it interpreted correctly, according to the will of his Father rather than the ideas of men.

But to 'fulfil' the Law also involved more than just providing a correct exposition. That was only the start. Conduct had to match. Only then could a rabbi be said to be fulfilling it. You could 'abolish' the Law in two ways: either by misinterpreting it, in which case you couldn't live it out correctly anyway, or by not living it out even if you did interpret it properly.

It is often overlooked that Jesus also mentions fulfilling the Prophets. This was not a matter of certain individual prophecies coming true in his life. The Prophets also provided guidance from God. They were teachers or Torah guides in their own way, and their words also needed to be 'fulfilled', in that their messages needed to be correctly understood and then taken to heart and allowed to affect behaviour.

Perhaps one reason why Jesus told the crowds not to think that he had come to abolish the Law was because some people were already thinking, and saying, that he was doing just that. By this time he was attracting a diverse group of people and accusations of this kind could have been starting to circulate. Certainly, some of the religious leaders would eventually be thinking this.

We have already commented in an earlier chapter on the verses from Matthew 5:21 onwards when considering the authority Jesus displayed ('you have heard that it was said, but I tell you'). Now we can see that in this passage he was also 'fulfilling the Law' by giving the interpretation God had originally intended. It is also important to realise that Jesus was not 'upping the standard' with his 'but I tell you' statements. This was always to have been the standard. Inward anger and lust was as much prohibited as any outward actions. If Torah is to be worthwhile as guidance and direction, then it cannot just be external. It must change us on the inside.

There is one other particularly Hebraic feature in these verses which needs our attention. This is when Jesus refers to the 'least of these commands' (v. 19). Which are these? And exactly what does he mean by this?

More literally this is a *light commandment*, a well-known rabbinic term for a commandment regarded as being of lesser importance. By Jesus' day the rabbis had decided which commandments were light in comparison to others, and tended to grade all six hundred and thirteen laws in this way. No commandment was light in itself, only in relation to another, and this same commandment might be heavy in relation to a third one. A heavy or weighty commandment was one to be taken more seriously than a light one.

A good example of this involves Deuteronomy 22:6-7. This states that if you come across a bird's nest with both mother and young in it, you may take the young or the eggs but you must let the mother go. This is set alongside the earlier commandment in Deuteronomy 5:16 to 'Honour your father and your mother' and is seen as light in comparison.

But why compare these two commandments anyway? How can this be justified? The reason the rabbis give is not just because of the obvious reference to a mother in both cases and the similar attitude involved, but because they both end with a common phrase, 'so that it may go well with you and you may have a long life'. This is seen to be the real link between the two, which makes comparison legitimate.

This illustrates another method used in Hebraic hermeneutics, called *gezerah shavah*, in which a verbal parallel is used to establish a link between two passages or, in this case, two laws. Here, the same promise of long life and prosperity is what connects these otherwise distant and distinct parts of Deuteronomy. Once such a link is found, the rabbis bring these two passages together for further examination and comparison. In this case, they decreed the bird's nest command to be light in comparison. You are still not to take (and presumably eat) the mother, but if you do, you have not done such a great wrong as this law is not as serious as that of honouring your mother.

This may seem quite reasonable to us, and perfectly natural to grade laws in this way. I suspect we all do this to some extent, both with the Old Testament laws and even with what we read in the New Testament, including the words of Jesus. But on what basis do we decide? And does God approve? Does he evaluate his own commands like this? It seems not, according to Jesus in Matthew 5:19, where he berates those who take the 'light' laws lightly.

It is interesting that the Mishnah records the words of a later rabbi on this matter. Yehuda ha-Nasi (c. AD 135-217) said, 'Be as mindful of a light commandment as of a weighty commandment, for you do not know the reward of each commandment' (Pirke Aboth, 2:1). He might have added, you don't know the punishment for each either!

As we now realise, here at the start of his ministry, Jesus is saying that he can be relied upon to correctly interpret Torah. As part of this, he states a key principle, namely that nothing is to be considered as less serious than anything else. Everything he teaches must be considered as equally important. When it comes to life in the kingdom there are no light laws, so don't think you can get away with breaking anything. In fact, true greatness comes from recognising this and living accordingly.

To summarise, here's another paraphrase, this time of verse 19. 'Anyone who breaks one of the so-called light commandments and tells others that it doesn't matter, will be called lightweight in the kingdom and regarded of low esteem. But whoever keeps these light commandments himself, and tells others to do so too, will be a heavyweight in the kingdom.'

The examples that follow in the rest of Matthew chapter 5 illustrate this point. Whatever Jesus' listeners had heard from others in the past regarding heavy and light commandments, this should be set aside in favour of what he is now telling them. For instance, murder and anger, even insults, are equally culpable; adultery and lust both break the same law.

As a final point on this, in Leviticus 19:17 we read, 'Do not hate a fellow Israelite in your heart.' The rabbis had declared this was light compared to the 'big' or 'heavy' commandment, 'You shall not murder' (Exod. 20:13, Deut. 5:17). It is interesting to see that at least one of Jesus' disciples had listened carefully to his own rabbi. John had set aside any such light-heavy comparison when he stated in one of his letters that 'Anyone who hates a brother or sister is a murderer' (1 John 3:15).

John had got the message. Have we? As we read through the laws in, say, Leviticus chapter 19 or Deuteronomy chapter 22, are we tempted to grade them in order of importance? Are we guilty of making some of Jesus' words of lesser significance? If so, then beware! We might be diminishing our significance in the kingdom of our rabbi.

Chapter Ten

Eye, Eye

Matthew 5:29, 38, 6:22-23, 7:3-5

In this chapter we will continue to look at some of the early teaching of Jesus found in Matthew chapters 5 to 7. We will consider several short passages with a common theme, that of eyes. The number of references to eyes in the Sermon on the Mount is quite surprising. A total of four, in fact. So the title of this chapter could be twice as long! Let's start with the most mysterious of these references and the one that needs most explanation from a Hebraic point of view.

Have a good eye!
(Matt. 6:22-23)

What is initially puzzling about these two verses is that they are contained within a passage that begins and ends with Jesus talking about money and our attitudes towards it (v. 19, treasures on earth; v. 24, God and Money, or Mammon). Why in the middle of all this does he suddenly seem to divert to something entirely different involving eyes, the body, and light and darkness? This can throw us completely unless we realise that he is still talking about money.

Once again Jesus is using a well-known idiomatic expression of his time when he talks about having 'a good eye' (*ayin tovah*) or 'a bad eye' (*ayin ra'ah*). Translations have struggled to come up with something suitable in English and all sorts of meanings have been attributed to what Jesus is teaching here, but quite simply someone with a good eye is a generous person, while someone with a bad eye is a mean person. Some versions nowadays do explain this in a footnote but still seem reluctant to make this part of the translated text itself. However, with this understanding of the idiom, we now see that this fits the context of money and could provide a meaningful lesson for us as his disciples. So let's explore this further.

It should be noted that the Hebrew word for 'eye' (*ayin*) is singular, as in the expression 'a good eye'. English translations find this use of the singular rather tricky and so have often opted instead for 'eyes' or even 'eyesight', but this destroys the original idiom. And even when the singular is used, translators have then struggled with 'good'. What is one good eye? As a result, several alternatives to 'good' are offered: single, sound, clear, healthy. But none of these really provide a meaningful solution, which is only to be expected when idioms are not properly transferred into a new language.

The 'good eye, bad eye' idiom was popular in ancient Judaism and is still in use today. Anyone seeking a donation for charity might shake a tin under your nose and say, 'Have a good eye!' What is happening here is that the physical concept of seeing is being extended to describe an attitude towards other people. Having a good eye suggests looking out for others by meeting their needs. Having a bad eye means being greedy, self-centred, blind to those around you. A good eye looks favourably on others. A bad eye focuses inward on yourself.

So how does knowledge of this idiom help us with these two verses? What exactly is Jesus saying here? Basically, how generous you are with your money affects the whole of your life, described here as your whole body. Generosity lights up your life and transforms everything about you. Being stingy, on the other hand, creates a sense of darkness. If we hold onto our money at all costs (being tight-fisted would be our idiom) then how little else of life can be grasped! But being open-handed with everything you own, generates a sunny disposition which others cannot fail to notice and benefit from.

It is not surprising to find these two Hebrew phrases in the Old Testament, especially in those nuggets of wisdom which make up Proverbs. In Proverbs 22:9 we read, 'The generous will themselves be blessed, for they share their food with the poor', where 'generous' is literally someone with a good eye. By sharing, not only does he bless others, he himself will be blessed. By contrast, in Proverbs 23:6-7, a stingy man, literally someone with a bad eye, is likely to eat alone as he 'is always thinking about the cost'. Another similar reference to 'a bad eye' is in Proverbs 28:22, where the stingy will find that in the end only 'poverty awaits them'.

Jesus also uses this idiom in the parable of the workers in the vineyard. The final verse (Matt. 20:15) is literally 'Or is your eye bad, because I am good?' where the Greek *opthalmos sou ponerous* is based on the Hebrew *ayin ra'ah*. Interestingly, the sentence ends simply with 'good' (*agathos*) with no further mention of an eye, as though this is implied by the earlier counterpart of a bad eye. It is noteworthy that translations, for once, usually render this correctly as 'generous', as though the idiom is understood in this context. Also the word 'envious' is a good choice to convey the meanness of some of the workers towards others.

There are also several places in the Jewish writings where this idiom is prominent. The Mishnah records the House of Hillel (an influential rabbi from the time just before Jesus) as declaring that, concerning the heave offering (*terumah*), someone who gives one fortieth of his income has a good eye, but a person who gives only one sixtieth has a bad eye (Terumot 4:3). Typically, the House of Shammai, a rival rabbinic school of around the same time, disagreed and set the 'good eye' amount as the even more generous one thirtieth!

Elsewhere in Jewish writings we are told that there are four attitudes towards giving. Two of them are described in terms of a bad eye. If you don't mind giving but persuade others not to, then your eye is bad towards what belongs to others. However, if you want others to give but don't do so yourself, your eye is bad towards what you own (Pirke Aboth 5:16).

Furthermore, in the Talmud, commenting on part of the Mishnah (Baba Bathra 4), there is a prolonged debate between rabbis on the sale or gift of property and what is or is not included. One rabbi, Aqiba, said that usually the seller sells with a good eye. Others held a contrary opinion, leading to the overall conclusion that only 'in the supposition of a good and bad eye is the point of their differing'.

At the risk of getting technical, it might be helpful to understand how the idiomatic phrase is constructed. And 'construct' is indeed the correct way of describing this, though that *is* getting too technical! Instead, we can think how in English we juxtapose an adjective and a noun. For us, 'good eye' would be read as a noun (eye) being qualified by an adjective (good). In Hebrew this is the other way round. It is read as 'good of eye', as the main component is 'good' and this is qualified by 'eye'. So, a generous man is good. But how is he good? In what specific way does his goodness present itself? The answer is, by how he acts upon what his eye sees.

In simple terms, having a good eye means we see the world in a good light. In particular we continually recognise how a good God is at work in his world. We recognise his hand of abundance, providing what we need. This encourages us to make a similar commitment to others. We give more of our resources and of ourselves. But a bad eye focuses on scarcity and lack, and sees a world in which everyone looks after himself, so the last thing we want to do is give. Instead we worry that we won't have enough for ourselves.

In that sense, our 'eye' affects our worry factor, so it is not surprising that immediately after this passage on money and generosity, Jesus goes on to teach about worry (Matt. 6:25-34). Worry is crippling, and stifles generosity. Why am I not generous? Why do I not give more? The reason is worry. If I give it away there won't be enough for me! The only way to store up treasure in heaven is by having a good eye.

Eye for an eye
(Matt. 5:38)

The second eye reference is in Matthew 5:38 where Jesus offers us a better way of combatting injustice than the system of proportional vengeance encapsulated in the phrase 'eye for eye, tooth for tooth'. This is found in several places in the Old Testament (Exod. 21:23-25, Lev. 24:19-20, Deut. 19:21), and originally had good intentions, the aim being to ensure that revenge did not spiral out of control. Matters would come to an end with the second 'eye'. Whether this was actually practised or not is open to debate, but anyway Jesus teaches a different approach for his disciples to follow (notice another one of those 'But I tell you' in verse 39).

The remaining verses in this short section (to verse 42) provide illustrations to back up Jesus' teaching 'Do not resist an evil person'. The first is rather dramatic. 'If someone slaps you on the right cheek, turn to them the other cheek also' (v. 39). Now that's an interesting one! When teaching this I often take the risk of inviting someone to do this to me – usually someone I know well! Inevitably, though, they end up slapping me (lightly!) on the *left* cheek, as they are right-handed (a risk I take, though I usually choose carefully!). The point being made is that it is difficult for a right-hander to strike the right cheek of someone standing opposite them. The only way is to use the back of the hand, which is not the natural approach. Think how in films a jealous wife lashes out at her lying husband. The impulsive reaction lands a blow on the left cheek. There is something a bit more pre-meditated about a back-handed blow, which can also indicate that a challenge is being issued, and a response is expected.

In the ancient world you would only interact with people with your right hand (the left was used for other purposes!). So this example from Jesus is a back-handed slap, which in the Roman world was how you hit a slave or someone of lower class. This isn't just about striking someone but about how you regard them. So if someone strikes you in a demeaning way, rather than fighting back, suggest they hit you like an equal. Give them the opportunity to reload and see what happens. They may repent or apologise. Or you may get another slap! That's what being a disciple of Jesus may involve!

The next example (v. 40) reflects the fact that in Jesus' day men had two basic garments: a simple tunic (*haluk*), which was a lighter robe, usually made of linen, worn when at home and at work, and a cloak (*tallit*), which was a larger rectangular cloth, usually woollen, which draped over the shoulders and reached down to the ankles. This gave protection from the cold and rain, and was the garment on which tassels were to be placed (Deut. 22:12). It was also used as a blanket at night, so if taken as a pledge, especially from a poor man, it had to be returned by sunset (Exod. 22:26-27, Deut. 24:12-13). Clearly, if you hand over both tunic and cloak you could be left shivering, something else to be prepared for if you are a follower of Jesus' teaching!

The next verse (v. 41) refers to the right of a Roman soldier to compel an able-bodied non-Roman citizen to carry his backpack for one mile (a thousand paces). To refuse could mean arrest and imprisonment, but at least Roman law restricted the distance to one mile. After that someone else had to be pressed into service. Naturally, people tried to evade this chore, but here was a further challenge Jesus gave to his disciples – if you have to do this, after a mile keep walking! This is another way for a disciple to show that he is prepared to obey Jesus' command, 'Do not resist an evil person' (v. 39). Exploitation should be repaid with kindness.

The final example (v. 42) is more intriguing. 'Give to the one who asks you, and do not turn away from the one who wants to borrow from you.' Is this a blank cheque? Are we really to give to everyone everything they ask for? Some understanding of the language that Jesus spoke will help resolve this.

In Hebrew, 'ask' has several meanings. For instance, you can ask a question, make a request, or ask to borrow something. The last of these seems to be correct here because of the parallelism involved, which means the second half of the verse should match the first.

In addition, there are different Hebrew words for 'borrow', with a subtle variation between their meanings. There are two kinds of borrowing. One is when we return the exact same item (a book or a car); the other is when we repay in kind (a pint of milk or ten-pound note). In this case, the item is consumed and then compensated for, replaced rather than returned. The different Hebrew words can reflect these meanings and so a poetic parallelism can be set up. But in English there is only one word to cover both kinds of borrowing, and so for variety the first is translated as 'ask', which tends to give the wrong impression.

It is also important to realise that this verse is still part of Jesus' teaching about 'an eye for an eye' and not resisting an evil person. Essentially, Jesus is saying, do not refuse to lend to someone out of retaliation. Do not take revenge by denying someone what they need when you can help out. This is not about getting out your cheque book for anyone who turns up on your doorstep. Rather, it fits within the context of the whole section, which shows us how not to become like the evil person but instead to reflect the attitudes and behaviour of our rabbi.

A plank in the eye
(Matt. 7:3-5)

The third 'eye' passage contains a certain amount of humour with its image of someone with a roof beam or plank sticking out of his eye trying to get near enough to someone else to point out the hardly noticeable speck of sawdust in their eye (Matt. 7:3-5). All this follows from the chapter's opening statement, 'Do not judge' (v. 1). But does this mean we are not to judge at all? Are we never to distinguish between right and wrong? How does this fit in with other parts of scripture which *do* seem to tell us to judge, especially other believers?

The key point is that this is a warning rather than an absolute command. Jesus is telling us to be aware that by judging others you are setting a standard that will be applied to you. This is outlined in verse 2, which contains a common saying that actually predates Jesus.

When it comes to judging it is motive that matters. We are allowed to judge but only in order to correct, not to condemn. And only within any authority that God gives us, otherwise we are usurping his authority. Above all we cannot judge people to determine their worth or eternal destiny. Only God can pass judgement on the value of others. This is the message of an earlier verse (Matt. 5:22), which contains warnings about what we say to each other. 'Raca' and 'You fool!' are not just terms of contempt but contain excessive judgements on someone's worth.

Generally, we tend to put other people down in order to make us feel better about ourselves, and this can affect our judgements. But we are allowed to judge if it helps put people right, lifts them up rather than squashes them. We must aim to judge without being judgemental.

Once again, Jewish writings often contain this important 'measure for measure' principle and express it in very similar words to those Jesus used. For instance, the Mishnah states, 'With what measure a man metes it shall be measured to him again' (Sotah 1:7). Also within the Mishnah is a warning from Hillel: 'judge not thy fellow until thou art come to his place' (meaning, stand in his shoes) (Pirke Aboth 2:5).

There are also references to such matter within the Talmud which employ the same imagery that Jesus used. For instance, 'If the judge said to a man, "Take the splinter from between your teeth", he would retort, "Take the beam from between your eyes"' (Baba Bathra 15b).

An even more striking similarity in language is found in a remark by Rabbi Tarfon, recorded in a commentary on Deuteronomy: 'I doubt if there is anyone in this generation who is fit to rebuke others. For if one says to another, "Remove the mote from between your eyes", the reply invariably is, "Remove the beam from between your eyes"' (Parashat Devarim).

The point of regularly quoting all these Jewish texts is to help us realise that Jesus fitted into the culture and customs of his day, while also providing an extra dimension which other rabbis may have lacked. What a privilege it was to have sat at the feet of rabbi Jesus!

Gouge out your eye
(Matt. 5:29)

The fourth place where the eye is mentioned is in Matthew 5:29. 'If your right eye causes you to stumble, gouge it out and throw it away.' In this dramatic passage, followers of Jesus may well wonder if self-mutilation is being prescribed. Are we to punish ourselves this drastically? Should there be lifelong consequences of a momentary wandering?

It may come as a relief to realise that Jesus is not speaking literally but using another Idiomatic expression that would have been understood as such at the time. Highly exaggerated hyperbole was normal among both Jewish and non-Jewish teachers when teaching about sexual morality. In both Rabbinic and Greek literature, overblown demands to cut off limbs from the body as a sign of seriousness about morality were commonplace. Jesus is simply using a contemporary metaphor to illustrate his teaching, rather than producing a new punishment. As his culture was familiar with this method of teaching, Jesus readily employed such picturesque statements in his illustrations.

But once we are relieved at the fact that this is symbolic rather than literal and that self-harm is not on the agenda, let's not forget that Jesus' language is intended to indicate once again the seriousness of these so-called 'lesser sins'. Keeping this sort of picture in mind is a good way of guarding ourselves against the possibility of losing our whole bodies in ultimate judgement.

Why is there so much on eyes in these chapters? Basically because the Hebrew mind prefers concrete ways of explaining something abstract. In particular, anthropomorphisms (attributing human characteristics or behaviour to God) are popular, so the human body and its functions feature regularly. These bring the message home and make it more personal.

In our next chapter we see what else we can glean from a Hebraic inspection of this famous sermon.

Chapter Eleven

The Show Mustn't Go On

Matthew 5:3-12, 6:1-18, 7:6

In this chapter we will look at more passages from the Sermon on the Mount, starting with the famous opening, that collection of sayings called the Beatitudes.

The Beatitudes

(Matt. 5:3-12)

When Jesus 'opened his mouth and spoke' at the start of the Sermon on the Mount, what emerged was a series of statements that have since been categorised as 'Beatitudes', from their common opening word, 'Blessed'. Why did he begin like this?

A rabbi's first lesson to his disciples was often a summary list of what he was going to teach, outlining his basic tenets and principles. These opening words of Jesus set out to define his teaching in many ways and prepare his disciples for what is to come.

One important feature of the Beatitudes is how they refer back to the Jewish scriptures. Jesus will be a teacher of

123

Torah, in its wider sense, so in these opening statements he wants those listening to know they can expect a continuity between what he will teach and the scriptures they have already learnt. He does this by providing many hints and allusions to Isaiah and the Psalms. How many would you recognise?

The phrase 'poor in spirit' (Matt. 5:3) hints back to Isaiah and those who are humble or 'contrite and lowly in spirit' (Isa. 57:15, 66:2b). The same prophet, in a famous passage on the year of the Lord's favour, also mentions comfort to all who mourn (Isa. 61:2, Matt. 5:4).

The meek inheriting the earth (Matt. 5:5) is almost a direct quote from Psalm 37:11, 'But the meek will inherit the land'. The Hebrew word *eretz* can mean the whole earth as well as just part of it. Jesus may well be extending the psalmist's thought from the land of Israel to something more worldwide.

Hungering and thirsting after righteousness (Matt. 5:6) alludes to Isaiah 55:1-2, while the pure in heart being able to see God (Matt. 5:8) should remind us of Psalm 24:3-4, 'Who may ascend the mountain of the LORD? Who may stand in his holy place? The one who has clean hands and a pure heart.'

Recognising similarities with verses from the Old Testament may also help us unlock the most puzzling of all the Beatitudes. The eighth Beatitude (Matt. 5:10) seems to suggest that persecution is something we should seek or at least welcome, and may even be a way into the kingdom. Does this really fit with the other seven Beatitudes? And how does it relate to what follows in verse 11?

The answer lies in realising that persecution can have two distinct meanings. It can be something unpleasant and hurtful done *to you*, or it can be something *you do*, as in pursuing something to the limit. We are more familiar with the first option and hardly consider the second at all in modern English, but in Matthew 5:10 the correct choice seems to be 'pursue'. Scholars agree this is a better understanding of the reflexive verb, and it also then links it back to Isaiah 51:1, 'you who pursue righteousness'. In this sense, to persecute righteousness means to chase after it and not give up or let go until you have achieved it.

As a similar illustration, consider how the word 'worry' operates in two ways. A sheepdog worries the sheep until it has got them where the shepherd wants. The dog does the worrying but the sheep are worried! Jesus said we are not to worry, meaning don't let other things worry you. But we can worry purposefully towards a given aim, provided we are not worried in the process! We do the hassling rather than getting hassled.

So Jesus wants us to persecute righteousness in the sense of pursuing it at all costs. If we do, then we will be blessed. This final Beatitude then reflects the first, with the common result of 'theirs is the kingdom of heaven', and parallels the fourth with its similar theme of hungering and thirsting after righteousness. Thus, Matthew 5:10 belongs with the first seven Beatitudes and forms a unity with verses 3 to 9.

This is better than coupling it with the following verse (v. 11), in which we find the other, more usual, use of 'persecute' which is something those who follow Jesus should expect, though they can feel blessed when it happens (provided it does so because they belong to him).

Another difference between verses 10 and 11 which sets them apart from each other is the change from 'those' to the more specific 'you', indicating a switch from those who are being encouraged to become part of the kingdom to those who are already followers of Jesus.

Having listened to how the Jewish Jesus began his initial teaching in the Sermon on the Mount, we now move on to consider one of the main words he used a lot in these chapters – hypocrite!

Take off that mask!
(Matt. 6:1-18)

Most people are aware that Jesus often accused the religious leaders of being hypocrites. The word features heavily in Matthew chapter 23, but there are also four references in the Sermon on the Mount (6:2, 5, 16, 7:5). What exactly is Jesus getting at here?

In modern parlance a hypocrite is someone who says one thing but does another. In Matthew 23:3, regarding the Pharisees and the teachers of the Law, Jesus warns, 'Do not do what they do, for they do not practise what they preach.' But in Jesus' day there was another meaning too. The non-alignment of words and deeds was just one aspect of hypocrisy. How you carried out your religious devotions was another. You could do and say the same thing, but if done for show then you were hypocritical. As Jesus also remarked, 'Everything they do is done for people to see' (Matt. 23:5).

Our word 'hypocrite' comes from the Greek *hypokrites*, which means an actor or stage player. In ancient Greek theatres actors wore large masks to represent the characters they were playing, and could swap them during a performance if they had more than one role. Pretending to be someone else is, naturally, what all actors do, but in Greek plays the skill was to interpret the story from behind a figurative mask through exaggerated movements and excessive sounds.

It is with this in mind that Jesus portrays those who make a show of their piety. In Jesus' time, there were three religious activities known as 'acts of righteousness' (Matt. 6:1), namely giving, praying and fasting. How should they be done? More importantly, how should they be *seen* to be done, or perhaps *not* seen?

Two words feature regularly in these verses: 'secret' and 'reward'. The opposite of putting your piety on show is to do it in secret where the only one who can see it is your heavenly Father (Matt. 6:4, 6, 18).

When it comes to giving, the contrast is stark. Trumpets were often used to announce certain actors as they came onto the stage so you knew who it was behind the mask. Was a trumpet, or shofar, actually blown in the synagogues and on the streets to publicise the act of giving (Matt. 6:2)? If so, this kind of theatricality was to be denounced.

Some, however, think that the mention of trumpets is a reference to the shape of the collection boxes in the Temple. More specifically, in the Court of the Women there were thirteen wooden boxes with trumpet-shaped bronze funnels to guide the coins into the box. The very recognisable noise made by the coins against the metal was called 'sounding the trumpet' and gave a good indication how much was being given. It was therefore easy to make a show of your giving by creating a lot of noise as you threw in your coins. We find this scenario in Mark 12:41-42, verses we will return to in a later chapter.

The reward for secret giving, and other inconspicuous acts of piety, is again contrasted by Jesus to that of the 'actors', who 'have received their reward in full' (Matt. 6:2), a phrase indicating that theirs is an immediate reward, like applause at the end of their show. But that is all it amounts to. Once they leave the stage it is all over.

Those whose piety is undertaken in secret are also rewarded now but it lasts longer and is to greater effect. English translations may seem to suggest this is purely in the future, 'will reward you' (Matt. 6:4, 6, 18), but this is because of the conditional nature of the statement: *if* you do this, then your Father *will* reward you. The 'will' is one of intent not delay. God will definitely reward you, and it will start straightaway. One aspect of this immediacy is that discipleship of this kind starts to change us from within at once. Moreover, 'hypocrites' get their reward from men, their audience, but disciples get theirs from the Father in heaven, which makes it future proof. Both are 'now' rewards, but one fades quickly, while the other goes on and on.

When it comes to praying, it is also inappropriate to turn it into a performance for public acclaim. Jesus' mention of going into a small room (Matt. 6:6; closet, in some versions) is intriguing as the homes of most people did not have enough rooms to allow for a separate one for prayer. However, the outer garment, the cloak or *tallit*, which we mentioned in an earlier chapter, could easily be thrown over the head and used as a covering to create a private or secret space for prayer.

Teach us to pray
(Matt. 6:9-13)

At this point in Matthew chapter 6 we meet the so-called 'Lord's Prayer', which also occurs in Luke chapter 11 where it is given in response to the disciples' request, 'Lord, teach us to pray' (Luke 11:1). This may sound as though the disciples had never prayed before, or had no idea how or what to pray, whereas they will certainly have been taught prayers from an early age both at home and in the synagogue. However, It was normal for disciples to look to their rabbi for further guidance in this matter. In this case, what Jesus gave his disciples was not a totally new prayer but a slightly updated version of ones they already knew, namely the Amidah and, more particularly, the Kaddish.

The Amidah (literally, 'standing') was recited at noon in the Temple and was considered obligatory. It is known to date back to before Jesus' time but there are ancient and modern versions. It has grown over the centuries to the point where it is now quite lengthy. However, it always followed the same format and is remarkably similar in outline to what we call 'the Lord's Prayer' but which should more accurately be referred to as 'the disciples' prayer'.

Detailed comparisons between these Jewish prayers and the prayer Jesus taught are beyond the scope of our studies. Those interested in knowing more can follow this up elsewhere. But it is safe to say that it is these prayers upon which Jesus based his reply to his disciples' request.

There are too many similarities for this not to be the case. For instance, the Amidah starts out with acknowledging God as Father and his place in heaven, and 'hallowed be your name' relates directly to the blessing in the third part of the Amidah.

However, there appears to be one main difference. Ancient versions of these Jewish prayers do not say much about forgiveness. Jesus seems to have added something extra or at least stressed it more. In Jewish thinking God could forgive, but here Jesus is inviting us to be like the Father in this respect. A radical concept indeed!

One familiar phrase in the Lord's Prayer is 'Give us today our daily bread' (Matt. 6:11). This is recited so easily that we may not stop to question the seemingly unnecessary repetition. Do we really need both 'today' and 'daily'? If we omit either one of them, won't it still mean the same?

Here is a translational puzzle that has baffled scholars. The Greek text contains a new word, *epiousion* (translated 'daily'), which appears nowhere else in the New Testament or among any Greek writings before the third century AD. The conclusion is that it was invented by the evangelists as they tried to convey something they understood from listening to the Jewish Jesus but had no existing Greek word to draw on. So 'daily' is not a proper translation, rather it is an attempt to say something that might be pertinent, and as such was chosen to fit 'this day', to re-emphasise that rather than add anything new, hence the strange doubling. But can we say anything about what it might be trying to tell us?

If we come across a new word we can try to work out its meaning by examining its structure. How is the word made up? Is there anything familiar about its components? Here we have *epi* and *ousia*. The latter comes from the verb 'to be' and so means 'being' or 'substance'. The prefix, *epi*, usually indicates 'on' or 'upon' but can also mean 'for', the precise choice being determined by context and grammatical factors. So knowing that it is something like 'for/on + being' may be helpful, without providing absolute clarity.

Another option is to look at a translation of the Greek New Testament into another ancient language that is closely related to Hebrew. One of the earliest of these is Old Syriac. This second-century translation takes Jesus' words and converts them back from the Greek into something close to his original language. In the Old Syriac version the expression *epiousion* becomes *lahmo ameno*, which implies bread that is perpetual, the 'never runs out' bread. This bread is all we need for now but with a promise of continuation.

This might be another useful guide, but if the disciples were listening to the Jewish Jesus, what might they have heard? Hebrew doesn't use many adjectives so this is not a description of a type of bread. 'Daily' bread is not a category of bread (like unleavened, crusty or sweet), not something we might find labelled on supermarket shelves. Hebrew is based on nouns and especially verbs. What something does is more important than what it looks like or is made up of, an emphasis summed up as 'function not form'. So this is about what bread is meant to *do*. It enables you to go on living from one day to the next.

Taking all these ideas into account, we could try our own translation! How about 'the bread which provides the onwardness of our being'. Or, 'the bread of our ongoingness'? Now who's making up new words?! Perhaps the gospel writers didn't do too bad a job after all!

As always, we should also look into the Old Testament for guidance. In Proverbs 30:8 we find a Hebrew phrase which is often translated as 'daily bread' but which more literally is the bread 'needful for me' or 'allotted to me'. The surrounding context, including verse 9, shows that this phrase refers to having just the right amount day by day, thus experiencing neither poverty nor riches, which reduces the temptation to sin, either stealing from not having enough or boasting and denying God through having too much. Could it be that this is at least part of the reason Jesus included this in the prayer he wants us to use?

Crossing over
(Matt. 6:2-4, 7:6)

Before we move on it is worth mentioning another feature that occurs here and elsewhere in the gospels – the chiasm (or chiasmus). In its simplest form, a chiasm of four items or words operates not in strict parallelism (A-B-A-B) but in a reversed form (A-B-B-A). So the first will be last and the last will be first!

The chiasm is named after the Greek letter *chi*, which looks like our capital X, hence the idea of two parts crossing over and becoming reversed. This device is commonly used to provide some structure to an account and to make it easier to memorise and restate. We meet a chiasm in Matthew 6:2-4, the section on giving. Although spaced out within a few sentences, there is a structural chiasm via the words reward – secret – secret – reward. Read these verses out loud, emphasising these words and you will hear it more clearly!

Another place where a chiasm is hiding in plain sight is in the strange statement about dogs and pigs in Matthew 7:6. 'Do not give dogs what is sacred; do not throw your pearls to pigs. If you do, they may trample them under their feet, and turn and tear you to pieces.'

Which of these creatures may trample something under their feet? Which may turn and tear you to pieces? Pigs do the former, and dogs do the latter, which sets up the chiasm: dogs – pigs – pigs – dogs.

But who are these dogs and pigs? Both are figures of speech used to refer to Gentiles, which accounts for the word 'dogs' occurring in the story of the Syro-Phoenician woman in Mark 7:24-30. This use of dogs (or pigs) to refer to people sounds derogatory today, even unacceptable to modern ears, but it was normal then, rather than disrespectful or disparaging.

Pearls also had a symbolic meaning, as in pearls of wisdom, or (more specifically in this case) teaching from the Torah. 'Stringing the pearls' was a way of describing how the rabbis put such teachings together.

So how are we to understand this rather isolated statement in Matthew 7:6?

Most likely Jesus was saying the Gentiles were not yet ready for such teaching. The faith of the Syro-Phoenician woman was an exception which may have been quite a surprise to Jesus. But basically Gentiles at that time could not be expected to keep God's Torah. They wouldn't know what to do with such teaching and the result would be unproductive (trampled on) or even painful (torn to pieces).

It is the same for us. Until someone has agreed to follow Jesus we cannot expect them to obey his teaching. We cannot force Christian morality and values on those who are not his disciples. If we try, we may get the opposite reaction to what we are hoping for, resulting in disappointment or hostility. As this evocative illustration demonstrates, pearls are not digestible. Pigs can't eat them, so they simply don't know what to do with them. How many pigs have you seen adorned with pearl necklaces? Trampling them into the mud seems the best option for these worthless items!

While we haven't looked at every word in the Sermon on the Mount, we have seen enough to realise how Hebraic it is. In particular, in this chapter we have learnt that when it comes to giving, praying and fasting, the show mustn't go on!

But we can't leave this important collection of Jesus' teaching until we understand how he ends it. In our next chapter we will encounter his first parable and dig deep into his whole strategy behind telling such stories.

Chapter Twelve

Dig Deep

Matthew 7:24-27

We have already seen in an earlier chapter how Jesus began his teaching ministry but how did he develop it? Was there a strategy? If so, what was the next step? Part of this answer comes at the end of the Sermon on the Mount, just before he closed his mouth and fell silent.

But before we look at the final few verses of Matthew chapter 7 we need to go back to the start and ask whether Jesus was teaching his disciples or the crowds, or possibly both. Clearly, if the crowds were amazed at his authority (7:28-29), they must have heard him. But a rabbi did not generally address huge crowds. He was not a mass evangelist or a Greek orator who loved preaching to the multitudes. If this is how Matthew portrays it then he must have a reason. What might that be?

We mustn't assume the Sermon on the Mount was a one-off occasion, a mega-event where Jesus wanted to deliver everything in one go and then retire for a few months. More likely these chapters are a compilation by Matthew of all the initial teaching of Jesus which took place in various locations in the Galilee over a long period. Jesus had already called some disciples but he was also attracting large crowds through his early ministry of teaching, preaching and healing. What would he do next?

In an earlier chapter we commented on how Matthew records that Jesus *sat* on the mountainside, indicating that here was a rabbi about to teach his disciples. We also read that 'his disciples *came to him*' (Matt. 5:1, italics mine). This expression indicates how a disciple committed himself to learning from his rabbi: he 'came to him'.

So the main focus of the Sermon on the Mount was to teach those who were already disciples. But there were crowds of other people too. Matthew wants us to know that Jesus was also teaching all kinds of people at this time. What he taught spread widely and became public. However, his aim was always to create more followers out of these crowds, more disciples who would *'come to him'*. So Jesus wanted to discover whether those who turned up in such large numbers were casual hearers or committed doers. To find out, Jesus ended by telling them a story, one which contained a big challenge.

The story in Matthew 7:24-27 is familiar to many, usually known as the parable of the wise and foolish builders though, as we will see, the parable of the two grounds would be better. The plot follows a simple outline with a clear outcome. The point is obvious: what will you do with what you hear? Will you take it seriously and put it into practice?

However, though the story may be relatively simple, some of the details require clarification. For instance, the images of sand and rock are carefully chosen, but not to suggest two different locations far apart, with someone deciding to build himself a beach house. Rather, this is about depth, laying good foundations by digging deeper through the sandy topsoil to the bedrock beneath. This is the only way to secure a building that will last. Equally, the only way to make sure Jesus' teaching doesn't disappear when it is most needed is to put it more deeply into our lives. How? By constantly living it out.

Moreover, if the correct image is sand (or sand-based soil) on top of rock, this may mean the two men are building their houses next to each other. They are going to be neighbours! The only question is how much effort they will take to get the foundations right. So this illustration can apply to two people next to each other in the crowd, or indeed two churchgoers in the same pew. They hear exactly the same teaching – but then what? The results can be very different.

Jesus has given some tough teaching in Matthew chapters 5 to 7, but now we know the true interpretations, now we have heard our rabbi 'fulfil the Law', now we have heard him say, 'But I tell you', then personal internal transformation must follow. This is what Torah (*any* Torah, *any* teaching) is meant to achieve. Hard work is now needed, but why take the easy option when disaster will obviously follow?

So Jesus is asking the crowds, '*How* have you heard me? Will you *do* anything about this?' He leaves them with a challenge to think about. Meanwhile, he will continue to focus on training his existing disciples, those who have already 'come to him'.

We will catch up with the crowds again later, but while we wait, let's scrutinise parables a bit more and see what we can learn. What exactly is a parable and how does it work?

Firstly, Jesus did not invent the parable. It has been claimed in the past that only Jesus could have created something so powerful and pertinent, but these views are now disregarded. So what is the origin of the parable? If Jesus did not invent it, where did it come from?

Basically, parables are rooted in both form and imagery within Jewish culture and their scriptures. A few examples can be found in the Old Testament, most notably the story told by Nathan to David to convict him of his sin regarding Uriah the Hittite (2 Sam. 12:1-4). There are several other passages which could also be said to prefigure the parables of Jesus (see the list in Appendix A). However, Jesus himself gave only one parable based upon an Old Testament text (Lev. 19:18) when he tells the story of the Good Samaritan.

What constitutes a good definition of a parable? Indeed, is there even one simple way of recognising a parable, or is it a broad term covering a range of scenarios?

Our word 'parable' is from the Greek *parabole* and the related verb *paraballo* meaning to 'set one thing beside another'. This translates the Hebrew *mashal*. Both words mean comparison, so the basic idea of a parable is a figure of speech in which a comparison is made, usually between God's kingdom and something in this world. The aim is to explain eternal transcendent realities in terms of something already familiar, often summed up in popular terms as an earthly story with a heavenly meaning!

When most people think of a parable they imagine a fairly long narrative, a sort of mini drama. Indeed many of the best-known parables are like that, such as the Prodigal Son or the Good Samaritan. But the word *mashal* is more flexible and includes a range of shorter utterances such as sayings, proverbs, riddles, oracles, fables and similitudes (using 'like' or 'as if'). In fact, it covers anything that is the opposite of plain or direct speech.

So asking how many parables Jesus taught can produce a wide range of answers, usually from around thirty to sixty. One way the total is boosted is to argue that in Luke 9:57-62 (a passage we looked at in an earlier chapter), Jesus' responses to the excuses given to him should be categorised as parables, at least in the sense of being enigmatic. So including these would add three more to the list and also show that the length of parables can vary considerably, the shortest being just a single sentence. A parable of medium length would be that at the end of the Sermon on the Mount, while there are some more very short cases in Matthew 13:31-33, 44-46. We will come back to these in our next chapter. Meanwhile, we note for now how smaller parables are often paired in order to boost the overall message. There is even an example of three parables being strung together along a common theme. In Luke chapter 15 the smaller parables of the lost sheep and the lost coin act as curtain raisers for the main event, the longer and better-known parable of the lost son (a better title than 'prodigal' son).

Certain features are commonly found, even expected, in parables. To be effective a parable must resonate with the listeners and draw them into the story from the start. This is why the characters are unnamed. It could be us! A parable also calls for a response and so is often left unfinished. The story stops but remains incomplete, asking us to provide the conclusion. Let's consider a well-known example. Imagine you've never heard it before – difficult, but try!

'There was a man who had two sons' (Luke 15:11). To a Jewish listener this opening would ring a few bells. Two sons? Many examples from Genesis come to mind: Cain and Abel, Isaac and Ishmael, Jacob and Esau. So, a man had two sons – hmm, that's not going to end well!

Then as the story progresses we should be asking ourselves, which son are we? The one who was lost in a distant land among the pigs, or the one lost at home, not fully enjoying his relationship with the father?

And then as the story ends we realise that it isn't really over. The father pleads with the stay-at-home son, desperate for him to come and join the party (Luke 15:28-32). We assume he refuses, but does he? The story doesn't tell us, because that's up to you! You provide *your* ending. What would you have done?

Another feature of a parable is the illogical behaviour that is often displayed, usually by the central character. In the above, the father gave away part of his estate while he was still alive and to his most irresponsible and wasteful son! Where is the sense in that?

There is often a shock involved too. When the younger son demands his share of the inheritance (and I want it now!) he is effectively saying to his father, 'I can't wait. I wish you were already dead'!

Shocks are commonplace in parables. In an earlier chapter we looked at a parable in which a king remarkably allowed a huge and unpayable debt to build up (Matt. 18:23-35).

And in another parable, that of the wicked tenants, the owner sends his son to his vineyard knowing that his servants have already been beaten and killed (Matt. 21:33-46, Mark 12:1-12, Luke 20:9-19). What is the owner doing? He's asking for trouble! But we find it is in the moment of shock that the real point is often made and we can learn the most.

So how should we interpret a parable? A common approach in the past was to treat them as allegories, stories where every single detail had to mean something specific. Everything was spiritualised, point by point, and milked for maximum effect. The worst example of this is St Augustine's commentary on the Good Samaritan (look it up for yourself if you're curious!). Thankfully, this approach is now redundant. Allegorical elements may still appear in a parable, but we should generally look for just one main point – usually a sharp one!

We have seen how Jesus fitted into the religious culture of his day, so we might expect to find many examples of parables from his contemporaries. Indeed, many do exist, though dating them with absolute certainty can be tricky. Jesus was definitely not the only Jewish teacher of his day whose methods included parables, though those we do have from this period tend to date from around the end of the first century AD, and seem to become more common from AD 70 onwards.

However, what is most interesting is not so much an exact date for these but the fact that there are several striking similarities between the parables in the gospels and others found elsewhere. The introductory formula is usually the same: 'To what shall I compare?' or 'It is like.' There are also common characters (rulers, masters, servants) and themes (banquets, journeys, business), and often the main point or application is identical.

Parables that are very similar to the one that ends Matthew chapter 7 have become quite well known today, and form a worthwhile comparison. For instance, here is an oft-repeated parable from Elisha ben Avuyah who flourished around AD 100.

'A person in whom there are good deeds and who has studied the Torah extensively, what is he like? A man who first builds of stones and then afterwards of mud bricks. Even if a large quantity of water were to collect besides the stones, it would not destroy them. But a person in whom there are not good deeds, though he has studied Torah, what is he like? A man who builds first of mud bricks and then afterwards of stones. Even if only a little water collects, it immediately undermines them.'

The resemblance is very clear but it is impossible to determine if Elisha ben Avuyah was influenced by what Jesus had said, or indeed if Jesus was influenced by any other rabbi he had heard. Priority is not the issue. Copyright doesn't seem to have existed in those days! Anyway, parables were primarily spoken and only written down later. So care should be taken not to make too much of this, but it does show the milieu in which Jesus operated and that other rabbis had similar concerns about how their disciples should live out what they had learnt. Like Jesus, they weren't afraid to issue such a challenge.

Here's another similar parable from the end of the first century AD, this time by Rabbi Eleazar Ben Azariah, found in a text we've quoted from before.

> 'A person whose knowledge Is greater than his deeds, what is he like? A tree whose branches are many but whose roots are few: the wind comes and uproots and overturns it . . . However, a person whose deeds are greater than his knowledge, what is he like? A tree whose branches are few, but whose roots are many. Even if all the winds were to come and blow against it, they could not move it.' (Pirke Aboth, 3:22)

What is important for us in these two examples is not so much the similarities with Jesus' teaching but the one big difference. Jesus does not refer to those who study Torah or who have knowledge, but addresses 'everyone who hears *these words of mine*' (Matt. 7:24, 26, italics mine). Jesus is placing himself and his teachings at the centre of this parable. Those listening would pick this up and once again be amazed at the authority he was claiming.

We have only started to understand the nature and form of a parable and how Jesus used this for maximum effect. There's lots more to come. So let's dig deeper.

If the parable of the two builders was the first one Jesus told, what was the second? And why?

Chapter Thirteen

Dig Deeper

Matthew Chapter 13

We ended the last chapter by asking that if the parable of the two builders was the first parable Jesus taught, then what was the second. But is this even a sensible question? How can we tell which was next?

In some ways, we can't. The gospels aren't written as chronological accounts. But there is a development in Jesus' ministry and Matthew in particular wants us to see how his teaching unfolded in method and purpose. So when Jesus ended the Sermon on the Mount with a story which left the crowds with a challenge, we are entitled to ask how he followed this up.

The answer is with another story, and a very similar one. This time, however, instead of two possible options, wise and foolish, there are four. And instead of two types of ground, sand and rock, there are four. This is the parable of the *four soils*, though it is usually called the parable of the sower.

We said in the last chapter we would catch up with the crowds again later, and of course they haven't really gone away. Jesus would always attract a crowd, but it is in Matthew chapter 13 that the next stage of Jesus' teaching ministry emerges. As before, large crowds gathered round him (Matt. 13:2), and once again Jesus 'sat' to teach them. First he sat by the lake of Galilee (Matt. 13:1), then in a boat on the lake, just off the shore where the crowds remained (Matt. 13:2).

Matthew chapter 13 is the main parable chapter of the gospel and is central to it in more ways than one. As with the Sermon on the Mount we might prefer to think of this chapter as another compilation by Matthew, summarising the next phase of Jesus' teaching. However, this time it seems that this may all have taken place on one busy day and that Jesus himself was responsible for how these parables flowed from one to another. But more important than this is to understand his strategy at this point, which once again centred on how the crowds might respond to him, and whether or not they were becoming disciples of his teaching.

At this point in his ministry, Jesus picked up his theme from the parable of the two builders, but now there are four options of how people might respond to his teaching. Instead of a simple wise-foolish dichotomy we have one good outcome that bears fruit in varying amounts and three that don't for various reasons (Matt. 13:3-9, 18-23).

Calling this the parable of the sower is to miss the point. The sower is the same in each case, as is the seed. The variable factor is the soils, so this is where the parable hits home. Nor is the story primarily about evangelism, about us 'spreading the word' to an unbelieving world, though this could be a secondary application. Rather it is once more about discipleship, how we as followers of Jesus receive the message he is teaching us about the kingdom. You are not the sower, Jesus is. You are one of these soils: path, rocky, thorny, good. But which?

We said before that a parable has to draw people in from the start. How does this happen here? Most translations have a reference to a farmer, for instance 'A farmer went out to sow his seed' (Matt. 13:3). It has commonly been taught that Jesus, sitting in his boat on the lake, suddenly saw a farmer on a distant hillside casting his seed all around, and being a good rabbi he pointed in that direction and drew inspiration from this real-life scenario to illustrate his theme. The problem with this is that it does not reflect life as it was then. In those days there weren't professional farmers with large fields. And anyway a farmer couldn't afford to waste so much seed. He would have been a lot more careful if he wanted to stay in business.

More in line with real life, then, is the fact that in the nearby Galilean towns and villages individuals had their own small patch where they kept their animals and tried to grow their own food. This was small-time cultivation on a local level. So everyone listening to Jesus knew what it was like to sow, and get it wrong! This is what drew them into the story. Their initial response would be, 'That's me! That happened to me recently!' Many times in their experience their seed would have fallen in less than fruitful ways. However, a knowing smile at the start was meant to change to a thoughtful frown once they realised the story was not primarily about them as a sower but as soil.

This point about the real-life situation of the parable is confirmed in the Greek text where the opening phrase is literally the rather ugly 'Behold, went out the one sowing to sow' (*Idou, exeilthen o speiron tou speirein*). Here again is a verbal repetition that highlights how the Jewish Jesus spoke in the original Hebrew. Our English versions again attempt to tidy this up, but do a disservice by including words that don't exist even in the Greek phrase at all. There is no mention of a farmer in the original, or even of seed, just a sower who sowed. The rest is implied; correctly in the case of seed, but wrongly regarding a farmer.

In this parable Jesus was again following a typical Jewish structure and methodology. Rabbis commonly used a four-part illustration. For instance, in our now-familiar source from the Mishnah we have:

> 'There are four qualities among those that sit before the wise: they are like a sponge, a funnel, a strainer or a sieve: a sponge, which sucks up everything; a funnel, which lets in at one end and out at the other; a strainer, which lets the wine pass out and retains the lees; a sieve, which lets out the bran and retains the fine flour.' (Pirke Aboth, 5:18)

Which one are you? Take your time . . .

A sponge soaks it all up, good and bad, and says everything is great without discernment. A funnel is the 'in one ear and out the other' student. A strainer keeps only the bad, whereas a sieve keeps only the good, so that's the best one! I'm glad the difference between a strainer and a sieve was illustrated, otherwise I might have got that wrong!

There are other similar sayings which also follow this pattern with four options along the lines of quick learner/ quick doer, quick learner/slow doer, slow learner/quick doer, slow learner/slow doer. I'll leave you to dance your way through all that! The point is that Jesus in the parable of the four soils was using a common template that his listeners would have recognised and known how to process.

This brings us on to the main objective of a parable, which was to enable the teacher to sort out the learners, or in our case for a rabbi to discern who the real disciples were and how they were getting on.

In Matthew 13:10 the disciples asked Jesus, 'Why do you speak to the people in parables?' As rabbis commonly did this it is rather a strange question unless they were really wanting to know why Jesus was doing this *here and now*. In particular, why was he using *only* parables when addressing the crowds? (See Matt. 13:34, Mark 4:34.)

The answer to this is wrapped up once again in the Jewish approach to teaching and the true intention of a parable. In Mark 4:33, we read that Jesus 'spoke the word to them [crowds], as much as they could understand.' Or, as they were able to hear it. In Matthew, Jesus seems to be saying they won't hear it, and quotes from Isaiah to back this up.

Is Jesus really saying he taught the crowds in parables so they wouldn't understand him? Well, yes! Sort of! A western teacher wouldn't do or say this, but it was fine for a first-century Jewish rabbi, for this was the function of a parable, its deeper purpose. It was for those who had 'ears to hear' and in particular for those who wanted to know more.

Parables are peculiar in that they both reveal truth and conceal it *at the same time*. That old adage that a parable is an earthly story with a heavenly meaning comes into play here. For some, it remains an earthly story. They won't get its meaning because they are not committed enough, not ready to become true disciples. For others, it reveals a truth that otherwise would not be grasped.

So Jesus always explained more to his disciples because they asked for more. They kept 'coming to him' (Matt. 13:10, 36). They would be able to understand what he was saying because they had already dug deep, built well, become good soil and were ready to bear fruit. Knowledge of the secrets of the kingdom of heaven had already been given to them (Matt. 13:11), so they could have more. They would get the meaning behind these stories (especially if they asked!) and then would do something with it. The crowds just got the stories.

This was perfectly normal practice in first-century Jewish circles. This was how a rabbi worked. It was not his task to make everything plain and simple at first. He aimed to hide treasure in what he said and set up a journey of discovery for the disciples. This was better than explaining directly and it was what his disciples expected from him. Digging deeper for the truth this way was ultimately more beneficial. It tested commitment and encouraged personal growth.

What if they didn't get it? They could always ask! And if they didn't ask? Then, like the unnoticed *remez*, their loss!

This was a general rabbinic method, but one that worked particularly well with regard to parables as they were designed to operate that way. Parables sifted those who heard them, and tested their hearing! In Hebrew terms, to

150

hear was more like our old-fashioned word 'to heed' which involved being attentive and determined enough to do something about what was heard. Here comes a parable – take heed!

We in the west today still prefer direct teaching. Tell us straight! But a parable is, well, parabolic! It is like being thrown a curve ball that we are expected to catch and run with. This is a deliberately more complex process but ultimately more rewarding and fruitful.

This also involved skill and hard work on the part of the rabbi. That is why Jesus' parables are so masterly and proficient, and such a key part of his teaching about the kingdom of heaven. A rabbi also had to recognise that not everyone would be willing to dig deeper and unearth the treasures he had put there. So, to be clear, Jesus isn't saying here that he doesn't want the people to understand him, but that he recognises not everyone will want to do the work necessary.

This is the same for us today. Many want to be part of a church but not as a disciple. The tendency then is to make our teaching cater to the lowest common denominator, whereas Jewish teaching caters to the highest. How many today want such a challenge? Some people don't, as they would then have to change, so their ears remain closed. 'Nice sermon, vicar', they might say as they shake hands on their way home until they turn up again next Sunday – but in the meantime . . .?

Every parable aims to provoke new thoughts, to challenge our current understanding, not reinforce what we already know. A parable is designed to perplex and prove difficult at first. It asks you to wrestle with it further. True disciples would want to discuss it afterwards. What their rabbi had said would be examined later in a group setting. Presumably that is what Jesus' disciples did. 'What did he mean? What do *you* get out of it? Hmm . . . perhaps we'd better go and ask!'

There are six further parables in Matthew chapter 13 which add to our understanding of how Jesus taught at this time. The structure of this section (v. 24-52) is fascinating. There are three parables for the crowds, then Jesus left them and went indoors, at which point his disciples joined him (*came to him*, v. 36) wanting an explanation of one of them, after which they received three more, just for them. Of these six, the first (weeds and wheat, v. 24-30) and the last (good and bad fish, v. 47-50) are similar, with two sets of paired parables in between (mustard seed, yeast, v. 31-33; treasure, pearl, v. 44-46). Let's examine these in turn.

The parable of the weeds and wheat is fairly straightforward, at least once explained (v. 36-43)! What might need clarifying for us is how the weeds could look similar to the wheat for a while. This is understandable if the enemy sowed something called bastard wheat. Only as the harvest drew near would the difference show as the wheat heads start to bow while the weeds stand upright. Meanwhile, damage has ensued with the roots of them all getting tangled up with each other. We may want to uproot the weeds but this is too difficult. This is a harvest-time job for the Son of Man and his angels. Meanwhile, we must live in a mixed world and wait for the end.

The parable of the mustard seed (v. 31-32) has similarities with the previous one. Again, something is sown and grows. This time not just any seed but the tiniest of all, and it grows into the largest plant in the garden. Is that the shock we have come to expect at the beginning of a parable? Not really! All that was well known.

What would have surprised Jesus' listeners was comparing a mustard seed with the kingdom of heaven, as the mustard plant was potentially a damaging weed. The root system was so immense and intertwined that no-one would plant one in their field. Indeed, it seems that at the time of Jesus there were laws prohibiting the planting of mustard trees beside certain other crops because of the threat it caused.

Then there is the curious way in which a garden *plant* becomes a *tree*! This is perplexing in itself, but in addition most types of mustard are only ever tall herbs, rarely reaching the height of a man. As such it remains a bush and, however large it may grow, it cannot become a tree. There are reports that the black mustard can achieve greater heights, even up to 3 or 4 metres. This was prevalent around the Sea of Galilee and in other parts of northern Israel, so perhaps Jesus had this in mind. It also has a small seed but can still hardly be called a tree in the way we think of one.

So at this point the parable does not make a lot of sense. What is happening here? Perhaps Jesus mentioned a tree as he wanted to introduce birds into the story. But why do this? To make a *remez*!

The link here is to Ezekiel, a book often used by Jesus for a *remez*. In Ezekiel 17:23 birds come to a tree to nest and find shade. In this vision, it is God himself who takes something small, a shoot or sprig from a treetop, and makes it grow into something large, a splendid tall cedar. This is what his people will become and how they will bless others. Now we see why the mustard tree appears in the parable, despite all its shortcomings. The kingdom of heaven is God's work and once it gets going it is unstoppable and hugely beneficial to all who will come into it.

Its partner parable (Matt. 13:33) also contains a surprise in that yeast usually represents sin, so for a rabbi to make such a comparison with the kingdom of heaven is also unexpected, even shocking. But the message is the same. Once yeast is introduced, you can't get it back out. Nor can you stop it spreading. It becomes all-pervasive.

Is there a *remez* here? Of course there is! This time the large amount of flour takes us back to Genesis 18:6. 'So Abraham hurried into the tent to Sarah. "Quick," he said, "get three seahs of the finest flour and knead it and bake some bread."' The Greek three *satas* in Matthew 13:33 is equivalent to the Hebrew three *seahs*, both about twenty-two litres or thirty kilograms! This is a huge baking project, but one which Sarah managed when three visitors unexpectedly arrived at their tent. The comparison with the kingdom becomes clear. It will expand and bless all comers. Just as the mustard tree welcomed visiting birds and Sarah provided generous hospitality to their guests, so too strangers and outsiders will find a bountiful welcome into the kingdom.

The other two short parables again act as a pair (Matt. 13:44-46). The common theme is that finding a place in the kingdom is a great joy and one worth giving up all else for. The rather strange start is why a man should be digging in a field that is not his in the first place!

The final story is usually called the parable of the net (Matt. 13:47-52) but a better description would be that of the good and bad fish, then it matches its counterpart, the wheat and the weeds. Once more this is about separation at the end of the age when eternal destinies are decided. How do we know which is a good fish and which is a bad fish? We don't, and we're not supposed to. It is not for us to sort out the catch. Once more, this is for the angels to do at the right time. Meanwhile, we catch as many as we can.

If these seven parables were all taught on the same day then it was quite an occasion. But before they could all retire for the night, Jesus had one final question for his disciples: 'Have you understood all these things?' (Matt. 13:51). On receiving a reply in the affirmative he told them that when their turn came to teach others about the kingdom, then they too should mix the known and the unknown. Remind people of what they should already know, but add something fresh as well. Parables are well suited to this.

PART THREE

Clues and Hints

Chapter Fourteen

The Yoke's On Me

Matthew 11:28-30

In the next few chapters we will explore more examples of how Jesus used the typical Jewish teaching technique called *remez*, a method which involved providing his listeners with a hint or allusion to another part of scripture in order to add extra depth and meaning to what he was saying. We start with Matthew 11:28-30, a short passage with a lot of Hebraic background to unpack, all of which will help us in our quest to listen more correctly to the Jewish Jesus.

The first important point to realise is that when Jesus says, 'Take my yoke upon you and learn from me' (Matt. 11:29), he is once again talking about discipleship. His use of words such as 'rest', 'weary' and 'burden' might make us think this is about taking time out from busy schedules or having a rest for a while as it's been tough recently. If we spend time with Jesus we will get refreshed and ready for action again. This might be what is needed at times, but is not what Jesus is saying here. The phrase 'taking the yoke' was associated with learning from a rabbi and referred to taking up discipleship.

The yoke was a commonly used image in the Jewish writings and culture of the time, especially when it came to following God and his laws. For instance, in Jeremiah 5:5 it is stated that the leaders of Israel knew the way of the Lord, the requirements of their God, but with one accord they had broken off the yoke. In particular, terms such as 'the yoke of the commandments' had become an expression for placing yourself under the Law.

Nowadays, a Jewish boy at the age of thirteen will take his Bar Mitzvah (literally, son of the commandment), a ceremony in which he declares himself ready and willing to come under the Torah. In terms of the Law he has 'come of age' and has effectively taken on the yoke of lifelong learning. Although the fully developed ritual didn't emerge until the thirteenth or fourteenth century, its origins can be traced back as early as the sixth century, and it is not unreasonable to suppose that something similar was in place around the time of Jesus as a means for a child to enter into adulthood, with all its responsibilities under the Torah.

Why was the yoke used to symbolise discipleship? The usual image conjured up is of two oxen ploughing a field. A young inexperienced ox could be yoked with a more mature one who had been doing the job for a while and was used to its demands. An experienced ox also knew what the owner wanted and how to obey his commands. By working alongside it, the younger one would soon learn what was expected. This is a perfect picture of the rabbi-disciple relationship that we looked at in earlier chapters.

Notice how at the start of this passage Jesus says, 'Come to me' (Matt. 11:28), which by now we should recognise as an expression for the way disciples related to their rabbi. They 'came to him' specifically to learn more from him. This opening phrase from Jesus is a further indication that this is about discipleship and sets the tone for the rest of what he has to say.

We should also realise that 'Take my yoke upon you and learn from me' is a parallelism, in which 'yoke' and 'learn' are matched in the two halves of the one statement. Effectively, Jesus is stating the same thing twice, not two different things. It could be rendered as 'take my yoke in order to learn from me'. Incidentally, 'learn *from* me' is a better translation than 'learn *of* me' found in some English versions.

So here Jesus is inviting us to yoke with him. He is the experienced one of the pair but is willing to partner with anyone who will admit to needing his teaching and be prepared to submit to his yoke.

Moreover, what Jesus is offering here is *his* yoke ('take *my* yoke'), not just the more general yoke of the Law. Typically, Jesus is centring this upon himself and his teaching. We saw this before, in an earlier chapter, when at the end of the Sermon on the Mount Jesus said, 'Everyone who hears these words *of mine*' (Matt. 7:24, italics mine). Here in Matthew 11:28-30, Jesus is declaring that his interpretation of God's Law *is* the Law. If we want to learn the true meaning of Torah, then we must be yoked to him and no-one else.

In particular, Jesus is offering us today a deeper learning experience than we can get from books or any human teacher. We can join in a living relationship with him, side by side, as we 'plough through life together'. We saw in an earlier chapter how we have 'one Teacher, the Messiah' (Matt. 23:10) and that we are not to call others 'teacher', even though some do have a teaching ministry within the body and we can learn from them. But, as we also saw before, they are not to make disciples for themselves, only more for Jesus. There is only room in the yoke for one Master, so make it the best!

Of course, all rabbis wanted their disciples, and indeed people generally, to take upon themselves the yoke of Torah by accepting God's reign over their life in obedience and dedication. But what should have been a positive experience often became a burden, which is one reason why Jesus criticised some of the Pharisees.

Note, *some* of the Pharisees, as there were several different kinds of Pharisee, and Jesus did not clash with them all. It is important to realise this was a broad movement with many well-meaning adherents within it. But of some, Jesus said on one occasion, 'They tie up heavy, cumbersome loads and put them on men's shoulders, but they themselves are not willing to lift a finger to move them' (Matt. 23:4).

The yoke analogy is found here in words like 'loads' and 'shoulders'. We also see in this verse how things sometimes weren't as they should be. Certain Pharisees created a burden by all their excess laws and wrong interpretations, so their yoke was heavy. Some even became known as 'shoulder Pharisees' for the way they piled extra weight on people so that, wearied by it all, they were tempted to give up. They were then categorised as 'sinners', a term which in the gospels simply means those for whom the Law was all too much and so had stopped trying.

Moreover, it seems these Pharisees were not prepared to 'yoke themselves' alongside people or assist them in keeping Torah. If they were not even willing to lift a finger it is clear they were not exactly 'putting their shoulder into it'.

By contrast Jesus said, 'My yoke is easy and my burden is light' (Matt. 11:30). This does not mean it was easy to follow Jesus. His teaching was still challenging, but being in his yoke would make it less oppressive and more fruitful. How could this be?

The answer lies in two comments Jesus makes about 'rest'. You've probably guessed by now that these both hint at the Old Testament. Here is the technique of *remez* being employed, as mentioned earlier.

For a start, the promise 'I will give you rest' (Matt. 11:28) is a direct quotation from Exodus 33:14, where the Lord assures Moses, 'My Presence will go with you, and I will give you rest.' It is noticeable that Jesus does not say that if you come to him then *God* will give you rest. By once again applying this directly to himself those listening might react, 'Surely only God can promise this!' So should this be regarded as a claim by Jesus to be God? Yes, in one sense, that is in the Hebraic sense of function rather than form. Rather than argue a case for his divine nature, he will simply do what God does.

It may be that some of his listeners picked up another small hint when Jesus referred to himself as 'humble in heart' (Matt. 11:29). In Numbers 12:3 we read that 'Moses was a very humble man, more humble than anyone else on the face of the earth'. So, some might exclaim, now he's comparing himself to Moses!

But there is another, more obvious, *remez* in the same verse (11:29), where Jesus said, 'You will find rest for your souls.' In Jeremiah 6:16 the exact same words occur and in a context that fits what Jesus is offering: 'Ask where the good way is, and walk in it, and you will find rest for your souls.' Jeremiah declares that when we walk in accordance with God's ways and laws, then our souls find rest. But when we stand at the crossroads undecided which direction to take, who will show us the right path? Whom do we ask? The answer is now clear. Being yoked with Jesus guarantees we take the right way, his way. Let him make the decision and feel the stress melt away!

This idea is also reflected in the true meaning of the word 'rest', which is not really an adequate translation. The Hebrew *menuchah* is literally a resting place or, perhaps more evocatively, a roosting place, where a bird settles for the night. Trying to sort life out and make all the right decisions is mentally exhausting. Our minds race around and get us into a flap. We need *menuchah* so we can stop 'flapping around' and find a place to roost.

Often our chapter and verse divisions are unhelpful, even misleading. At times we should ignore these numerical distractions and read on. Keep following the text and you might find further connections. So just because Jesus has stopped speaking at the end of chapter 11, it doesn't mean that we should stop reading there. Is it coincidence that in chapter 12 there are so many references to that greatest 'rest' of all, Sabbath (Matt. 12:1, 2, 5, 8, 10, 11, 12)? The word keeps jumping out at us – seven times in all! In fact, eight times in the Greek, as 12:5 is literally 'desecrate the Sabbath', not 'the day'. Has Matthew arranged it like this because one of the greatest burdens the Pharisees had to their yoke was all those extra Sabbath laws? When we listen to what Jesus has to say on this topic, his yoke is light in comparison.

Further into the New Testament we realise the importance of replacing the previous yoke that had burdened the Jewish people with the new one of Jesus. In Acts chapter 15 we read how the early church had to come to terms with Gentiles being converted and with all the related issues, such as whether they should be told to keep the Jewish Law. Peter is emphatic about this: 'Now then, why do you try to test God by putting on the necks of the Gentiles a yoke that neither we nor our fathers have been able to bear?' (Acts 15:10). The point being that Jewish converts to Christ had now received an easier yoke, so surely this must be the right one for Gentile converts too.

Paul tackled a similar issue with the converts in Galatia. 'Stand firm, then, and do not let yourselves be burdened again by a yoke of slavery' (Gal. 5:1). Basically, why be burdened with something heavy from the past once you have been set free and given Christ's yoke instead?

The particular yoke that a rabbi presented to his disciples could also be thought of as the way that he interpreted Torah, and was usually shown by his answers to several important questions that all rabbis were asked. The main question was 'What is the greatest commandment?' Just about every rabbi would say that this was to love God (as in Deut. 6:5), but they didn't always agree on what was the second greatest. It was this answer which then became one of the main ways of defining a rabbi's yoke.

Naturally, Jesus was asked this question and at first responded as expected, before adding, 'The second is like it: "Love your neighbour as yourself"' (see Matt. 22:35-39). You may have wondered why Jesus seems to give a supplementary answer (based on Lev. 19:18) when he was asked only for *the* greatest commandment. Now you know. He was defining his yoke in this way, which all his disciples would then be expected to take up.

Jesus was not the only one with this particular yoke. The famous rabbi Hillel agreed that 'Love your neighbour' was the second greatest commandment. His main rival, Shammai, however, said that it was to observe the Sabbath. His yoke was based more on obedience rather than love, though 'Love your neighbour' would have been somewhere on his list, and Hillel would also have had Sabbath observance as part of his yoke. Both love and observance of the Law were regarded as important but when two commandments clashed and you couldn't obey both at same time, then that was when your yoke came into play and helped you decide what to do.

One such example involved a stricken donkey which had fallen due to its heavy load, sometimes known as the problem of the Donkey in the Pit. Helping your neighbour when his donkey was in trouble was part of the Law (Exod. 23:5, Deut. 22:4) but so was not working on the Sabbath. So what if this donkey problem occurred on a Sabbath? The effort needed to help would violate the Sabbath. A real dilemma!

From their yokes, as explained above, you might expect Shammai to say leave the donkey until tomorrow, and Hillel to say rescue it now. However, Shammai made an exception in this case so everyone was happy – especially the donkey! The point for us is that Jesus used this agreement to counter those criticising him for healing on a Sabbath (Matt. 12:11, Luke 14:5). Jesus' yoke involved showing love whatever the day of the week. They would rescue an animal on the Sabbath so 'how much more' (a typical rabbinic way of proving a case) should he heal a more valuable human being. Point made! Critics silenced!

We said earlier that the yoke was a commonly used image in Jewish writings, so let's end this chapter with a couple of examples from one of the best-known books of the Apocrypha. Ecclesiasticus, also known as the Wisdom of Jesus Son of Sirach, or Ben Sirach for short, has a lot to say on the importance of wisdom and how to get it.

'I opened my mouth and said, Acquire wisdom for yourselves without money. Put your neck under her yoke and let your souls receive instruction; it is to be found close by.' (Ben Sirach 51:25-26)

Incidentally, did you notice the Hebraic way in which this began?

Another passage earlier in the same book is worth quoting at length.

'Listen, my child, and accept my judgement; do not reject my counsel. Put your feet into her fetters and your neck into her collar. Bend your shoulders and carry her, and do not fret under her bonds. Come to her with all your soul, and keep her ways with all your might. Search out and seek, and she will become known to you; and when you get hold of her, do not let her go. For at last you will find the rest she gives, and she will be changed into joy for you. Then her fetters will become for you a strong defence, and her collar a glorious robe. Her yoke is a golden ornament, and her bonds a purple cord. You will wear her like a glorious robe, and put her on like a splendid crown.' (Ben Sirach 6:23-31)

Texts such as these are interesting in their own way and provide pre-echoes of expressions used by the Jewish Jesus. But of course, it is the wisdom of his yoke that we need most of all, so let's continue to listen to him as he drops more *remez* into our expectant ears.

Chapter Fifteen

The Green Tree

Luke 23:31

We have already established how profitable the *remez* can be as part of a rabbi's method of teaching. By a shrewd choice of words, which can also be found within their scriptures, he can stimulate the thinking of his disciples and provide them with more to reflect on than is immediately apparent from his own words. Such hints to texts they already know supply a wider context for a rabbi's own teaching, which will then reinforce or extend his message.

Sometimes a single word was sufficient. On other occasions a phrase was more beneficial. In each case a rabbi was providing his listeners with clues which drew on their lifetime of reading and memorising the scriptures. This also worked when addressing those not within his immediate circle of followers, as nearly every Jewish person at the time had a sufficient grounding in these texts to be able to pick up the references and make the connections.

As we begin to look at more of these clues, we will start with an extraordinary example given in the most distressing of circumstances.

In a verse that is unique to Luke's Gospel we come across a puzzling remark: 'For if people do these things when the tree is green, what will happen when it is dry?' (Luke 23:31).

When we read these words we might suspect that this is a quote from somewhere. Perhaps it is a proverb or saying? Certainly there is some imagery involved which needs explaining. Let's look at this first before applying it to the situation in which the words were spoken.

The *remez* here is to a verse in Ezekiel, a favourite book of Jesus when it comes to providing such hints. In Ezekiel 20:47 we read of trees 'both green and dry'. Does this help? We need the full context to appreciate all that is being said here.

Ezekiel chapters 20 and 21 tell us about Israel's rebellion and how God will respond in judgement. Here is a prophecy against Jerusalem and its Temple in which the fire of judgement will be so fierce that it will burn up the green trees as well as the dry. Normally, trees that are still green have enough sap and life within them to survive the heat that completely destroys those nearby that are lifeless and parched. But in the most intense of fires, no tree can withstand the heat. That is the picture here. 'I am about to set fire to you, and it will consume all your trees, both green and dry' (Ezek. 20:47).

But what do these two kinds of tree represent? Fortunately we have a further explanation in Ezekiel. The prophet complains to the Lord that no-one will believe him: 'They are saying of me, "Isn't he just telling parables?"' (Ezek. 20:49). Ezekiel realises his listeners might get the earthly story but not the heavenly meaning! As a result the Lord speaks to Ezekiel again with a parallel prophecy, so we should ignore the chapter division and read on!

In this next section the image of setting fire to trees has changed to that of drawing a sword, and 'consume' is now 'cut off' (Ezek. 21:2-5). The parallelism of this passage with Ezekiel 20:46-48 shows us that the green trees are the righteous and the dry trees are the wicked. Now we know what all this means we can return to Jesus' statement in Luke 23:31 and see how to understand what he wanted to say.

We should perhaps consider first of all whether those who heard Jesus would have made the link to this passage in Ezekiel. It might seem obscure to us but would not have to them, especially as it contained a simple analogy in story form that made it more memorable. In addition, it was about the crucial matter of judgement and a prophecy that had already come true.

It is also worth noting that the use of the word 'green' to mean 'supple' or 'living' occurs only a handful of times in the scriptures, and when combined with 'tree' or 'wood' this number reduces further. So there was little chance of ambiguity or confusion, especially as the occurrence in Ezekiel is the most relevant.

Another point is that just before speaking these words, Jesus directly quoted in full a verse from Hosea also on the theme of judgement. 'They will say to the mountains, "Fall on us!" and to the hills, "Cover us!"' (Luke 23:30, Hos. 10:8). Perhaps Jesus intended this as a sort of warm up, to attune their ears ready for the more hidden reference.

(Incidentally, are your ears sufficiently attuned to pick up from Hosea 10:8 an allusion to a later verse in the New Testament (Rev. 6:16)? Perhaps more importantly, when reading Revelation would you have heard the hint back to Jesus, and also back to Hosea?)

Now let's consider what Jesus is saying in Luke 23:31. Who or what is the green tree? Is this a person? Ezekiel has shown us that the green trees are righteous people, so we can deduce that here in Luke this is also a person, and in particular a righteous one. Can we presume that Jesus is referring to himself? Does this make sense?

The phraseology appears a little awkward in certain English translations that have *'when'* the tree is green or dry. This is misleading as it might seem to be referring to a particular tree that is green at times and dry at others. It also misses the main point. The Greek text is literally *'in* a green tree'. This accurately reflects the Hebrew idiom being used, which means 'to do to'.

So as a whole the phrase is better rendered as 'if men do these things *to* a green tree, what will they do *to* a dry one?' This meaning becomes more obvious as the same was said by Jesus concerning John the Baptist after he had been beheaded: they 'have done to him everything they wished' (Matt. 17:12). Jesus goes on to add in that passage that in the same way he would suffer at their hands.

So the righteous green tree is Jesus. And he speaks these words after he has been condemned to death as a traitor to Rome. This is what 'men will do to him'. In fact, he is already on the road to the site of his crucifixion, having been flogged and physically mistreated in many ways. At this point Simon from Cyrene is carrying Jesus' cross, giving him some respite, just enough for him to be able to give a short message. We see here how the power of a *remez* allows Jesus to speak volumes when under extreme duress and with no time to quote the whole passage from Ezekiel and give a full sermon on its application.

So what about the dry tree, the wicked person or people? Some think this could refer to the Romans. If Pilate could sentence to death someone whom he had acknowledged as innocent and in whom he repeatedly declared he could find no fault (John 18:38, 19:4, 6), then what might be expected to happen to Pilate or the Romans in return?

However, the Romans are more likely to be the 'men' who are doing 'these things'. In which case the dry wood are the Jewish people who would also suffer at their hands in due course. One day they too would experience the terrible vengeance of Rome, something which did indeed happen in AD 70 with the siege of Jerusalem and eventually the complete destruction of the Temple.

That the dry trees are the Jews not the Romans makes more sense as Jesus is addressing those immediately in his presence, following him on his way to Golgotha. In particular he notices the wailing women who typically formed part of the crowds that surrounded those heading towards their execution. Turning to them he calls them 'Daughters of Jerusalem' (Luke 23:28) and suggests they direct their weeping towards their own fate and that of their children.

'Daughters of Jerusalem' may just be a way of referring to them as inhabitants of the city, but it is possible that by mentioning Jerusalem Jesus is giving a preliminary hint to the Ezekiel prophecy as this was specifically about Jerusalem and the sanctuary there (Ezek. 21:2).

More relevant, though, is the fact that only a few days before, when Jesus was approaching Jerusalem for his final week there, he wept over it. He did so not because of what was about to happen to *him*, but because of what would happen to *them* in years to come, all because they didn't 'recognise the time of God's coming', that the Messiah was in their midst (Luke 19:41-44).

Their weeping for him may have reminded Jesus of his weeping for the city. 'If you, even you, had only known . . .' (Luke 19:42). Now it is too late. Judgement is inevitable. Not because they 'killed Jesus' (the Romans did that) but because they hadn't recognised him as Messiah, and so they had lost that which would have brought them peace.

To summarise, Jesus is saying that if this is happening to me, a green tree, innocent and righteous, then how much worse will it be for you dry trees when the Romans turn their vengeance on Jerusalem. One can only imagine what horrors await you, so turn your weeping away from me and towards yourselves and your children.

There is another significant point to be made from this extraordinary verse. Was Jesus hinting one more time that he was their Messiah? The title 'Green Tree', or 'Righteous One', had become a Messianic description. When Messiah comes this is what he will be like, how you will be able to recognise him. Perhaps in this *remez*, with all its hints and allusions, Jesus was providing them with a final chance to realise what they had previously missed.

It is worth concluding this chapter with one more connection of our own. Something similar comes across in Peter's first letter when he writes: 'For it is time for judgement to begin with God's household; and if it begins with us, what will the outcome be for those who do not obey the gospel of God?' (1 Pet. 4:17).

Is there a resemblance here with Luke 23:31, again showing how Peter had learnt from his rabbi? Peter then continues the thought with his own quotation from the Old Testament (though from the Greek version known as the Septuagint, if you wonder why it is not exactly the same in our versions): 'If it is hard for the righteous to be saved, what will become of the ungodly and the sinner?' (Prov. 11:31).

In our next chapter we shall be investigating a double *remez*. Two clues for the price of one. Or maybe even three, if our ears are really well tuned.

Chapter Sixteen

The Temple, The Temple, The Temple!

Matthew 21:13, Mark 11:17, Luke 19:46

In this chapter we focus on just one gospel verse, a familiar one where Jesus refers to the Temple as a house of prayer that has been turned into a den of robbers. This verse is found in all three synoptic gospels and contains a very powerful example of the use of *remez*. Here we have not only a double hint to the Old Testament scriptures, but even a clue within a clue taking us back still further in time and giving an even more striking message to those who heard Jesus.

So who did hear him on this occasion? All three gospel writers place this event at the same time and place. The location was the Temple, in particular the area where the moneychangers and merchants were making their large profits on behalf of the priestly authorities and at the expense of the people. The specific moment in time was shortly after Jesus had entered Jerusalem for his final week and, more precisely, just after he had expressed displeasure and even anger at what was going on in the Temple area by overturning the tables of those involved and driving them out.

So these words of Jesus were heard by many people. There were the usual crowds thronging around the Temple area who 'hung on his words' (Luke 19:48) and were, once again, 'amazed at his teaching' (Mark 11:18). Then there were the chief priests and teachers of the Law whose reaction was rather different. They 'began looking for a way to kill him' (Mark 11:18).

Why did a few simple words make such a stir? Because, as always, those listening heard much more. They knew the texts to which Jesus referred and, more importantly, the full passages from which they came, and so they could catch his broader message with all its accusations and implications.

The double *remez* begins with a few words from Isaiah. Jesus makes it clear that these are not his own words. 'It is written', he declares, and then follows this with a snippet from Isaiah 56:7, but enough to make the whole of Isaiah 56:1-8 resonate in their minds. Centuries earlier Isaiah had described the purposes God had envisioned for his Temple, in particular its role as 'a house of prayer for all nations'. The last three words ('for all nations') are found only in Mark's account but everyone who heard Jesus would have been able to complete the quotation for themselves. They also knew that Isaiah had spoken these words as part of a longer prophecy about salvation for others outside of Israel, foreigners whom God would also gather to himself and who would bind themselves to the God of Israel.

Let's hear in full two verses from this chapter.

'And foreigners who bind themselves to the LORD to serve him, to love the name of the LORD, and to worship him, all who keep the Sabbath without desecrating it and who hold fast to my covenant – these I will bring to my holy mountain and give them joy in my house of prayer. Their burnt offerings and sacrifices will be accepted on my altar; for my house will be called a house of prayer for all nations.' (Isa. 56:6-7)

This was God's vision for his house, the Temple. He wanted everyone, including non-Israelites, to feel at home there, but it was failing to be what he intended. In modern phraseology it was no longer fit for purpose and a dreadful advert for Judaism which was bringing God's name into disrepute! Only Jesus says all this much better with a second *remez*!

This time he draws on another prophet, Jeremiah, who in a previous era had also stood in the same place as Jesus and thundered out a message from the Lord concerning Israel's sins and their consequences.

'Has this house, which bears my Name, become a den of robbers to you? But I have been watching! declares the LORD.' (Jer. 7:11)

We might wonder if Jesus paused slightly between the first and second *remez*. The gospel texts suggest he went straight on. But perhaps he took a second to look around and then, with a sweep of his arm or an accusing point of a finger, he continued, 'But *you* ...'

By simply saying 'den of robbers' (just two words in Hebrew), Jesus fired an arrow deep into the minds of those around him. The result would be to bring to the surface all the surrounding verses and more. But what exactly was the deeper message they heard?

Jesus turned a rhetorical question in Jeremiah into a direct indictment. But was he just addressing the vendors and their dishonest practices, which were tantamount to daylight robbery? In fact, they were merely symptomatic of a larger problem, and that is reflected in the context of the second *remez*, the whole of Jeremiah chapter 7.

The heading for this chapter is usually along the lines that false religion is worthless in God's sight. His people were not living in a righteous way and yet they assumed that because they had the Temple they were 'safe'. They believed it was a guarantee of God's continual favour whether or not they kept his laws.

So Jeremiah was instructed by the Lord to stand at the gate of the Temple and proclaim: 'Do not trust in deceptive words and say, "This is the temple of the LORD, the temple of the LORD, the temple of the LORD!"' (Jer. 7:4).

This reiteration of 'the temple of the LORD' had become a mantra which, by being repeated often enough, deceived them into thinking they could live as they liked, including worshipping other gods, and that the Temple would act as a form of insurance policy to protect them. But this was far from the case. They would only be allowed to 'live in this place' and so have a Temple at all, if they reformed their ways and actions (Jer. 7:3, 7). This was God's house. It was designed to bear his holy Name, so it was his decision whether or not they would have a Temple, or even be allowed to stay in the land he had given to their ancestors.

God instructed Jeremiah to make this clear: 'Will you steal and murder, commit adultery and perjury, burn incense to Baal and follow other gods you have not known, and then come and stand before me in this house, which bears my Name, and say, "We are safe" – safe to do all these detestable things?' (Jer. 7:9-10).

Immediately after this comes the verse which Jesus quoted to trigger in the minds of his listeners all that Jeremiah was saying here. But they would also know that Jeremiah chapter 7 didn't stop at verse 11. This was a very long chapter, the rest of which contained an even stronger indication of what would happen to them if they didn't mend their ways. And to get this across, Jeremiah himself had started with a *remez*!

In Jeremiah 7:12, we are told, 'Go now to the place in Shiloh where I first made a dwelling for my Name, and see what I did to it because of the wickedness of my people Israel.' That reference to Shiloh might test our biblical knowledge a little, but those in Jeremiah's day knew exactly what he was referring to and what had happened there. And those in Jesus' day knew that this was a key part of that chapter of Jeremiah and that Jesus intended them to include this in what he was saying. So let us go now to Shiloh – and refresh our knowledge.

Shiloh was the religious capital of Israel during the time of the Judges and was where the tabernacle resided for around three hundred years. It was thus the first place where the tabernacle became a permanent structure, and within it was the Ark of the Covenant. Shiloh was also where the Jewish people would gather for the main festivals. Hence God's description of Shiloh as the place where 'I first made a dwelling for my Name' (Jer. 7:12).

But Jeremiah adds, 'See what I did to it because of the wickedness of my people Israel' (Jer. 7:12). This is a reminder of how the sanctuary at Shiloh was destroyed and the Ark captured by the Philistines. Here is a *remez* back to 1 Samuel 4:10-11, and hence to the full story behind these verses. Here it is, in brief.

The priest at the tabernacle at that time was Eli. He had two sons, Hophni and Phinehas, but they were wicked men who 'had no regard for the LORD' (1 Sam. 2:12). They abused their priestly privileges and so God's anger flared against the corruption of the priesthood of the day. Through an unnamed 'man of God' a prophecy was given that both sons would die on the same day, bringing the House of Eli to an abrupt end (1 Sam. 2:13-36).

That day eventually came, a day on which the people of Israel were defeated by the Philistines and lost four thousand men in battle. That in itself should have told them something. At least they asked the right question: 'Why did the LORD bring defeat on us today before the Philistines?' (1 Sam. 4:3). But instead of waiting upon the Lord for an answer they took the Ark of the Covenant from Shiloh and into their battle camp, assuming this would '*save us* from the hand of our enemies' (1 Sam. 4:3, italics mine).

What was their thinking in doing this? Were they treating this sacred object as *their* insurance policy, a sort of lucky charm? Might they have even chanted, 'The Ark, the Ark, the Ark – we are safe!'? A bit of speculation here, no doubt, but if this was in their minds then what followed next could be regarded as inevitable.

The Philistines responded by fighting more vigorously and inflicted an even heavier defeat upon Israel who lost another thirty thousand men. The Ark was captured and Eli's two sons died as predicted. When the news reached the elderly Eli, he fell off his chair and died of a broken neck. Meanwhile, his daughter-in-law, Phinehas' wife, went into labour and died in childbirth, but not before naming her new son Ichabod, saying, 'The Glory has departed from Israel' (1 Sam. 4:4-22).

Well, that was quite a day! It's not difficult to imagine that these events would remain long in the collective memory of the Jewish people and be easily brought to mind by those who heard Jeremiah when he hinted at this (in Jeremiah chapter 7), and indeed later when people heard Jesus' allusion to that same chapter of Jeremiah. It is also worth noting that this episode in their history was repeatedly kept alive in Jewish memories in one of the longer Psalms of Asaph (see Ps. 78:56-64). It appears that perhaps the Psalms weren't always just pleasant songs to provide enjoyable times of worship!

Incidentally, it seems the Philistines completely destroyed Shiloh as part of their campaign. Perhaps that's why we don't remember it so much. But it left an indelible mark on the Jewish mind and when Jeremiah started using this again as an example of what could happen to Jerusalem and the Temple, he was seized and threatened with death (Jer. 26:1-9). Such was the potency of the allusion to Shiloh.

Meanwhile, back to Jesus. His 'den of robbers' reference points in one clear direction. Those listening, both the crowds and the religious leaders, are left in no doubt that he is declaring judgement on the priesthood for the way they are running the Temple. As a result, God's anger would be poured out on Jerusalem and its fate would be similar to that of Shiloh.

The link with the passage in Isaiah would add to the impact of the message. Not only would they lose the Temple but God's plan to bring salvation to other nations would go ahead regardless.

This example of linking two passages in this way was also a known rabbinic technique called *gezerah shavah*, or a comparison of equals. If two passages shared a common word or short phrase, they could be brought together for comparison and to see if they shed light on each other. In this case, both Isaiah 56:7 and Jeremiah 7:11 have 'house' in common (as a reference to the Temple). In fact, 'my house' is found in both, at least if you're using the Septuagint version of Jeremiah.

One final point, just in case you're thinking this is all very interesting but it can be safely left in the historical archives of Judaism. It can't apply to me – can it? Have you never been tempted to do something less than godly and thought to yourself, 'I go to church, go to church, go to church. I'm safe!'? Then listen to your rabbi hint otherwise.

Chapter Seventeen

Breakthrough!

Matthew 11:12

In this chapter we are concentrating on Matthew 11:12. This violence-fuelled verse has not only proved troubling for those reading the scriptures but also head-scratchingly troublesome for translators and commentators. A great deal of violence is apparently connected with the kingdom of heaven, which doesn't seem appropriate, so many varied and contorted attempts have been offered to explain it differently. Should we somehow tone it down or should we seek to clarify how such force is justified? Consensus is elusive. Perhaps what we really need is a 'clue' to provide a breakthrough.

As we look through various translations, the early Authorised Version dramatically announces, 'And from the days of John the Baptist until now the kingdom of heaven suffereth violence, and the violent take it by force.' The New King James Version is only marginally more helpful by updating part of it to 'suffers violence'. The Revised Standard Version has 'suffered violence, and men of violence take it by force' and the English Standard Version is very similar.

However, when we come to the New International Version we find early editions tell us 'the kingdom of heaven has been forcefully advancing, and forceful men lay hold of it', which is quite different. More recent editions of this translation change this to 'the kingdom of heaven has been subjected to violence, and violent people have been raiding it', with the original phrase 'been forcefully advancing' relegated to a footnote. So this is already getting a bit confusing, not just in the choice of words used but in the way the verb changes between passive and active. Troublesome indeed!

It's time for some Greek. This is going to get a bit technical in places, but stay with it and all will become clear – eventually!

The Greek verb involved is *biazo* which means 'to inflict violence' or 'to apply force', especially with regards to a forced entry. It also has the sense in modern Greek of 'to hurry' or 'be in a rush', indicating speed or strength of movement. In the text in Matthew we have two related words: *biazetai* (a verb) for the clause concerning the kingdom of heaven, and *biastai* (a noun) for the violent or forceful men in the second part of the verse.

The main debate is over *biazetai*, whether this should be in the passive voice (the kingdom suffers violence) or the active voice (it advances violently). In simple terms, in the first case, something *is being done to* the kingdom; in the second, it is the kingdom itself *which is doing* something.

Grammatically, this is also described using the terms transitive and intransitive. A transitive verb only makes sense if it is exerting the action on an object. An intransitive verb does not need an object, and then there are some verbs which may be used both ways. You've probably guessed by now, *biazo* is such a verb! (Another is *baptizo*, which we will come across in a later chapter when discussing the baptism mentioned in Luke 12:50.)

Scholars also talk of middle or deponent voices, where a deponent verb can be passive in form but active in meaning! Clearly there can be ambiguity contained within the intricacies of translation. Those interested in such discussions can follow this up at their own leisure. For now we just need to know there are two different approaches to translation. Is the kingdom suffering violence or inflicting violence? And this choice will affect how we read the second part of the verse.

If the former is correct (the kingdom is suffering violence), then the violent men (*biastai*) mentioned must be the ones inflicting this violence upon the kingdom. Who might these be? Commentators have made several attempts at answering this. They could be the religious leaders of Israel, or the Romans, or maybe even demonic spiritual forces. Perhaps it is a reference to misguided and impatient Jews, such as the Zealots, who were seeking an aggressive way of bringing the kingdom in. Then there is Herod Antipas who has just had John the Baptist beheaded. John was the first to suffer from violent men in this way but others in Herod's mould would follow.

In each case the motive is to stop the kingdom advancing. Here is a rising opposition of evil men (or spiritual forces) who are out to do harm, and those proclaiming the kingdom, or already living in it, are being treated violently. Many say this is the more normal meaning for *biastai*, namely that men of violence are attacking the kingdom to stop it growing. In which case 'the kingdom of heaven is suffering violence' should be the correct rendering.

But others take the opposite view. Rather, it is the kingdom that is advancing strongly, and these violent men are those who are zealously embracing it. Bold and triumphant, they take hold of the kingdom with fierce determination to drive it forward even more forcefully. In this case, who might these violent men be?

Firstly, there is John the Baptist with his dynamic preaching and radical lifestyle, together with the huge crowds that thronged to hear him and responded to him. Then there are the exorcisms and mighty miracles of Jesus himself, and also the disciples who are already being sent out with authority to repeat the works of their master.

There is even the thought that we should include those who are doing violence to their own sinful lives by serious repentance and putting their old nature to death. And then there are those whose evangelism is doing battle on behalf of the kingdom by snatching people from the evil kingdoms of this world. Both are advancing the kingdom in their own particularly dynamic way, but not by any kind of physical violence towards others, which would actually do nothing to further the cause of the kingdom.

We should also take into consideration the similar verse in Luke's Gospel. In Luke 16:16, we read, 'Since that time, the good news of the kingdom of God is being preached, and everyone is forcing their way into it.' Luke also employs the same Greek word, *biazetai*, but uses it to describe the manner in which people are entering the kingdom as a result of hearing the good news.

The opening 'Since that time' also relates back to John and is similar to Matthew with his reference to 'from the days of John the Baptist until now', but the rest is rather different. There is no sense at all of physical violence in connection with the kingdom of heaven. Rather it is preaching the good news that is advancing the kingdom. Moreover, the word (verb) *biazetai* is reserved for individuals to describe how they are rushing into the kingdom in their eagerness not to miss out.

It is difficult to be sure if these two gospel accounts are related variants of the same statement or whether they reflect two separate occasions. Luke's version appears in a string of rather disconnected 'additional teachings' and without the same overall larger context about John the Baptist that Matthew provides. Perhaps Luke's account helps a little to understand what Matthew wrote, but we are still left with lots of conflicting options. We need a breakthrough! We need a clue!!

As usual it is by listening to the Jewish Jesus that we can hope to find our way out of this difficulty. What Hebrew word might he have used? Is there a *remez* here?

The Greek words under discussion here have Hebrew equivalents that are based upon the root p – r – tz. (In general we find such equivalents through the Greek translation of the Hebrew scriptures, known as the Septuagint. In particular, *biazo* is the Greek translation of *paratz*.)

A good illustration of the use of such Hebrew words is found in Genesis 38:29 which describes the unusual birth of Perez, one of the twins born to Judah and Tamar. As the two boys struggled to come out of the womb, a tiny hand emerged but then drew back, which gave an opportunity for his brother to become the firstborn.

The text comments that when Zerah drew back his hand, his brother Perez came out (*paratzta*), at which point the startled mother observed, 'So this is how you have broken out!' or 'What a breach (*paretz*) you have made!' We then learn he was forever to be known as Perez, or in Hebrew Paretz, which means 'breach' or 'breaking out'.

As well as being a birthing term, this Hebrew word can refer to anything that 'bursts forth' forcefully, such as water bursting a dam. Here we can see an association with an action that can appear violent or even explosive. But the expression also became commonly used within shepherding, and it is here we find our *remez*.

At the end of Micah chapter 2 there is a passage about the return of the remnant of Israel from exile, and how God will gather them together like sheep in a pen. It is in the last verse that the key words occur which provided Jesus with a *remez* for his comment on the kingdom of heaven.

> 'One who breaks open the way [*ha-poretz*] will go up before them; they will break through [*partzu*] the gate and go out. Their King will pass through before them, the LORD at their head.' (Mic. 2:13)

This verse is full of imagery. The 'one who breaks open' is called the breaker or breach-maker, and refers to the shepherd who breaks open the pen to release his sheep who then 'break through' or burst forth.

A shepherd would pen up his sheep for the night in a temporary enclosure made of rocks. He might build a makeshift wall against a hillside or use a cave, or there may be some existing stone walls nearby. Once the sheep are inside, the shepherd closes the breach. In the morning he pulls aside some of the rocks and creates an opening.

Now sheep don't usually form an orderly queue! In this case, they can hardly wait! Once released they burst through the gap, several at a time, pushing and shoving, most likely expanding the breach in the process, perhaps with help from the shepherd who would knock aside more stones with his staff. Having been set free or 'birthed' in this way, the sheep rush headlong after the shepherd, their 'redeemer' who has made the breakthrough for them. For the rest of the day they will gladly follow closely, with him 'at their head'.

The scene overall is one of the joyful movement of a large and expanding group. Initially applied to Israel's return from exile under God's gathering and leading, Jesus now picks this up to depict the kingdom of heaven as bursting forth like sheep from a pen. This is the correct image, not one either of suffering violence or of inflicting it.

Moreover, there are no violent men taking anything by force. Rather, as a consequence of the kingdom breaking out in this fashion, those who 'lay hold of it' are themselves experiencing a breakthrough in their own lives in terms of salvation and personal freedom. And as they surge through this newly made breach like a tide of water bursting through a dam, they make it even wider, sweeping others into the kingdom along with them. This image is also compatible with the similar statement in Luke 16:16, which we looked at a little earlier.

So when the Greek words are turned back into Hebrew and compared with Micah 2:13, we find we can make more sense of what Jesus is saying about the kingdom. But there is something else to understand.

Jesus states that the kingdom of heaven has been breaking forth 'From the days of John the Baptist until now'. By making this time reference Jesus is indicating that it was John who had forced open the breach. His radical preaching for a change of lifestyle together with his call for a baptism of repentance had opened up a new way. It is thanks to John that a strong movement had broken out and was now bursting forth in life-changing power.

But in the Micah text there seems to be only one person who fulfils all the roles. The breaker who releases the sheep and who 'will go up before them' is the same figure as the king who 'will pass through before them', and who is also to be recognised as 'the Lord at their head'. Moreover, while in his *remez* Jesus establishes that John has performed the role of the breaker it is clear John cannot fulfil the rest of the Micah text. He is now in prison by order of Herod Antipas. He cannot be the King figure. Who then is this?

It has to be Jesus himself, but it is noticeable that Jesus does not directly speak of himself either as the King or as Lord. He wants others to make that extra connection, and conclude that he is their expected Messiah. Would others see that what John started, Jesus is continuing as people now flock to him?

Finally, in Matthew 11:14 Jesus equates John with the Elijah to come, someone whom the scriptures declared to be the messenger who would prepare the way before the Lord (see Mal. 3:1, 4:5-6; also Isa. 40:3, Matt. 3:3). It is notable that rabbinic sources often refer to a two-person fulfilment of Micah 2:13 in which the breach-maker is Elijah, and 'their King' is the Branch, the Son of David. One such source, found in a commentary called the *Metsudat David*, is worth quoting in full.

> *'The breaker goes up.* Before they go up, the one who breaks through thorn fences and prickly hedges goes up before them in order to clear the way. Thus, it is said concerning the prophet Elijah that he will come before God's redemption to direct the hearts of Israel to their father who is in heaven, to be a gateway to that redemption, as it is said, "Behold I am sending the prophet Elijah and he will turn the hearts of fathers . . ." (Mal. 4:5-6). *They break through.* Those returning from exile also will break through fences and hedges and pass through the breach as if it were a gate and a way by which they can leave the Exile, that is to say, they will have the courage to turn to God in repentance, and as a result, they will depart the Diaspora. *Their king passes on before them.* As they return their king will pass on before them. He is the King Messiah. He will march at the head of them all, for at that time he, too, will restore his Shekinah to Zion.'

That's quite a long passage and tricky to follow as a whole if you are not used to reading Jewish commentaries, but I hope you can see that some of the details in it are in line with what we have been discussing.

In this chapter we have had to work hard to establish the meaning of a difficult text, but it is worthwhile in the end.

We are discovering that when we listen to the Jewish Jesus a breakthrough often emerges, so let's continue in this fruitful vein as we seek to shed light on other tricky passages.

Chapter Eighteen

The Son and The Stone

Matthew 21:33-46, Mark 12:1-12, Luke 20:9-19

Let's start with a joke!

'I tell you that out of these stones God can raise up children for Abraham.' (Matt. 3:9)

Now this may not have you rolling around on the floor in hysterics or chortling away for hours. I guess you really had to be there. And be Jewish. Or at least someone with a fair smattering of Hebrew.

But what was the occasion? And who was the joker? And whom was he trying to get laughing?

The answer is John the Baptist speaking to some Pharisees and Sadducees somewhere in the Desert of Judea near to the Jordan River.

But why did he say *that*? Was it *meant* to be that funny?

John was making a pun on 'stones' (*ebanim*) and 'children' (*banim*), which is where your knowledge of Hebrew would have helped. And it was a follow-up to his previous statement to the Pharisees and Sadducees who were coming to where he was baptising, when he said to them, 'And do not think you can say to yourselves, "We have Abraham as our father"' (Matt. 3:9). That's why you probably had to be there. Context is everything.

Now you've got the point of this serious piece of humour, store it away for later. Meanwhile, let's turn to another of Jesus' parables, one about some tenants in a vineyard (Matt. 21:33-46, Mark 12:1-12, Luke 20:9-19).

Vineyards often featured in rabbinic parables, frequently as a metaphor for Israel. Moreover, the introduction of an absentee landlord into the story would also have been familiar. Here was a real-life scenario, as attested by historical records and papers which show such business arrangements, including examples of failed attempts to collect what was due and of the servants who were sent to make the collection being thrown out of town. However, in Jesus' version something even more dramatic is to take place!

The way Jesus begins this story is to drop a big hint to a passage in the prophets. We now know this is a *remez*. But which part of the Old Testament was meant to register in the minds of those listening?

The opening of the parable would have immediately triggered a response. Words such as vineyard, winepress and watchtower all draw attention to Isaiah chapter 5, known to us as The Song of the Vineyard, in particular to verses 1 to 7. Here we learn how vines are grown on the Judean hillsides, which are very fertile but full of rocks and stones. These have to be cleared first and are often then used to build a wall to define the plot or make terraces.

Thistles and thorns might also be put on top of the stones to keep out small animals. Other stones would be used to build a watchtower which can be lived in during harvest time. After that you would dig a place for a winepress nearby. Then, when all was ready, you could sit back and wait for a good crop!

So far Jesus has set up his story with something familiar from the scriptures. But not many of his listeners would have been landowners of this kind so he introduces the idea of tenants to draw them more fully into the narrative. As we have already said, this would have been a typical scenario. A wealthy owner might live some distance from his vineyard; at harvest time a certain percentage of the fruit would be due to him so he would send others to collect his entitlement. In the culture of the day these servants carried the identity and authority of their master, so to maltreat them was equivalent to abusing the owner himself.

In Jesus' story the servants were repeatedly beaten and killed, so the owner, as a last resort, sends his son. But once he has been murdered the owner has a decision to make. What will he do now? Jesus includes this question to get his audience more involved in the story. What would *they* do? But that question would also take them back again into Isaiah chapter 5. The *remez* was still at work. They would have known exactly what the owner would do as they recalled verses 4 and 5: 'What more could have been done for my vineyard than I have done for it? . . . Now I will tell you what I am going to do . . .'

God now starts to dismantle his vineyard, step by step, working back through the building process. He removes the hedge of thorns and thistles, then breaks down its wall. Finally, he commands the clouds not to rain on the ground so it becomes an uncultivated wasteland.

This is judgement, stage by stage. God has been longsuffering but ultimately has to act.

Jesus' parable has the same feel. The situation gets more and more serious with no change of heart from the tenants, so it must also end in judgement. In Matthew's account those listening are in no doubt how to reply to Jesus' question. The owner will bring those wretches to a wretched end, and he will rent the vineyard to other tenants, who will give him his share of the crop at harvest time (see Matt. 21:41).

Notice, by the way, another typical Hebraic doubling with both 'wretches' and 'wretched end'.

Jesus picks up their reply and drives home the point of the story, just in case it hasn't been fully understood: 'Therefore I tell you that the kingdom of God will be taken away from you and given to a people who will produce its fruit' (Matt. 21:43).

But it is important to note carefully at this point what he is and isn't saying. We need to look back to where this section of teaching begins and who is involved. Jesus is in the temple courts and the chief priests and elders of the people come to him, questioning him on his authority (Matt. 21:23). So when he says the kingdom will be taken away from *you* he is referring specifically to the religious leaders, not the Jewish people as a whole. Jesus has already told the leaders that others such as tax collectors and prostitutes are entering the kingdom of God ahead of them because they believed the message brought by John the Baptist. Even after the leaders saw this happening they did not repent or believe.

The parable of the vineyard which then follows sets out to reinforce this message. It is clearly aimed at the religious leaders, and they knew it. 'When the chief priests and the Pharisees heard Jesus' parables, they knew he was talking about them' (Matt. 21:45). Moreover, when Jesus adds that the kingdom will be given to 'a people', he is not suggesting that it will be given to the Gentiles instead of the Jews, rather to people in general, both Jews and Gentiles, all who will receive it and become fruitful vines.

But is this the main point of the story? Where is the real sting in the tale? Not necessarily in the tail! We usually expect a story to build to a climax with the focus at or near the end. But we have already seen that the Hebraic way of thinking is not so much linear as symmetric about a central pivot. We noted in an earlier chapter that this is called a chiasm (remember those dogs and pigs?!). Chiastic form places the focus in the *middle* of the story. In this parable there is not only the expected outcome at the end when the vineyard is taken away from the tenants, but there is a huge shock halfway through: 'Last of all, he sent his son to them' (Matt. 21:37).

What is the owner thinking of? Surely he realises what will happen? He knows what they've done to his servants, so presumably he can anticipate their reasoning and subsequent actions. How could he be so foolish and reckless with the life of his son? But he goes ahead anyway. This is where the bombshell drops.

We have already seen how parables describe excessive behaviour and portray characters acting in remarkable and foolhardy ways. In this case even the tenants seem to lack common sense. Didn't they realise the owner had the power to come and destroy them? Did they really think they could inherit the vineyard this way?

The overall intention behind such exaggerated scenarios in parables is to heighten the tension and intensify the reaction of the hearers. When the owner runs out of servants to send and turns to his son instead, the story reaches a dramatic climax.

At this point in the story there is a further significant detail found in both Mark and Luke. In these accounts, when the owner says he will send his son, he adds 'whom I love' (Luke 20:13; also Mark 12:6 where it is in reported speech, 'whom he loved'). This not only imparts extra poignancy to what is about to occur but acts as another resonating *remez*.

In Genesis, God tested Abraham over his willingness to offer his son Isaac as a sacrifice. Abraham was not to know that the angel of the Lord would intervene at the last moment to prevent this when he initially heard God say, 'Take your son, your only son, *whom you love . . .*' (Gen. 22:2, italics mine). In Jesus' day, everyone would have known this famous story and made the connection.

Fewer, however, would have heard the voice from heaven announce something similar about Jesus at his baptism, 'This is my Son, whom I love' (Matt. 3:17). And only three were privileged to hear this again at his transfiguration (Matt. 17:5). But in each case the link with the parable would suggest that, unlike Isaac, this son will not be spared. In fact, as with the owner's son, his death would be planned and brutal.

Now we have established the centrality to the story of a son we can return to that rib-tickling quip, admittedly more serious than funny, which opened this chapter. John's wordplay between stones (*ebanim*) and children (*banim*) is now repeated by Jesus in the singular. Jesus has already mentioned the son (*ben*), now he ends with the stone (*eben*), by quoting Psalm 118:22-23 (Matt. 21:42).

Why does Jesus refer to this particular Psalm here? Not to show off his pun-making wit, but because of the common theme of rejection. Both son and stone suffer in this way, but in each case it is not the end of the story.

Eliminating the son did not produce what the tenants were hoping for. In fact, it led to something far worse, including their own demise. And the rejected stone became even more important, whether you read it as capstone or cornerstone. In both cases God had plans that couldn't be thwarted. As the Psalm states, 'The Lord has done this', and the result is a marvel to behold.

The point is now well made. Rejecting and eliminating Jesus will not further the purposes of the religious leaders. Their problems will not end but increase to the point of their own downfall. Meanwhile, the son-stone will rise to greater heights and increase in magnitude.

Are there any more helpful hints back to the Old Testament? Perhaps. This might make you think of Nebuchadnezzar's dream in Daniel chapter 2 where a rock smashed to pieces a mighty statue before growing into a huge mountain. Also worth noting is that in later rabbinic tradition, Psalm 118:22-23 is seen as a commentary on the well-known story of Samuel anointing David (see 1 Sam. 16:1-13). When Samuel goes to Jesse's household to anoint Israel's future king, Jesse presents seven of his sons but the youngest, David, is out in the fields tending sheep. The son Jesse had rejected was to become Israel's greatest king.

One final point. Jesus rounds off this section of teaching with an intriguing extra comment concerning the stone. 'Everyone who falls on that stone will be broken to pieces, but anyone on whom it falls will be crushed' (Luke 20:18; see also Matt. 21:44). Once again this reflects a Jewish saying of the time: if a pot falls on a rock, woe to the pot; if a rock falls on a pot, woe to the pot! Final score: Rock 2 Pot 0.

We have not quite finished looking at the many *remez* that Jesus gave in the course of his teaching. We have one more collection of clues to consider in our next chapter.

Chapter Nineteen

Give Us A Clue

In this chapter we will take a quick glance at a few more occasions when Jesus added depth to what he was teaching by an appropriate reference to the scriptures. Let's see how many of these clues we can pick up.

Paying taxes
(Matt. 22:15-22, Mark 12:13-17, Luke 20:20-26)

The challenge levelled at Jesus over paying taxes to Caesar is a familiar part of the gospels, as is his famous reply about rendering unto Caesar the things that are Caesar's. But what did this actually entail and is there a *remez* for us to find?

This incident is one of the test questions that Jesus faced during the last week of his life. A great deal happened in that week and it is a worthwhile exercise for any Bible student to make a list of every event and teaching that took place from the time of his triumphal entry into Jerusalem until the moment of his arrest. A large proportion of each gospel focuses on those few days, because what happened in them is particularly significant.

In this case we have another attempt to 'catch him in his words' (Mark 12:13). What is interesting is who tried to do this. Some of the Pharisees came together with the Herodians to lay this particular trap. These two unlikely bedfellows were complete opposites within the spectrum of Jewish opinion. As their name suggests, Herodians supported the dynasty of Herod and didn't oppose the political set-up of the time. In this they were more akin to the Sadducees, but here in opposing Jesus the Herodians and Pharisees were more aligned.

The issue they brought to Jesus was not really about paying taxes as such. Rather, it concerned the matter of offering tribute to Caesar and the use of a coin to do so. The Greek shows that Luke uses a different word (*phoron*) from Matthew and Mark (*keinson*). Both seem to refer to a kind of poll tax, something levied on individuals or property rather than goods or income, but the essential meaning of *keinsos*, from which *keinson* is derived, is tribute money. The coin involved was specifically 'the coin of tribute', which was Roman money, not Jewish. Indeed, the Authorised Version does translate this correctly with, 'Is it lawful to give tribute unto Caesar, or not?' and 'Shew me the tribute money' (Matt. 22:17, 19). This is how we should understand Jesus' request to 'Show me the coin used for paying the tax' (Matt. 22:19). The alternative 'Show me a denarius' (Luke 20:24) also makes this clear, and that is precisely what was brought to him.

What was special about such a coin? It was not for paying taxes in the sense that we do today, rather it could be used at certain places to buy incense which you could offer to Caesar as a tribute. It seems Herod had built three temples where this could happen. You took your tribute coin to one of these and exchanged it for a pinch of incense which you used to show your devotion to Caesar.

There were varying attitudes towards this among the Jewish people and religious groups. The Herodians were quite happy doing this, the Pharisees less so. In fact the Pharisees were rather split. Some said it was idolatry, others believed it was acceptable, just part of the way the world was at that time. The Sadducees went along with this practice, but unsurprisingly the Zealots and Essenes were vehemently against it. It is not unreasonable to suppose that those Pharisees who joined forces with the Herodians on this occasion believed it *wasn't* acceptable, so that Jesus was faced with opposing views. He was being set up to fail, as he was bound to upset someone!

It was therefore quite a moment when Jesus asked them to show him such a coin. Was this a clever move intended as a delaying tactic? Roman coins were not permitted on the Temple Mount so one would have to be fetched. Or was his aim to show up the division between his accusers? Which of *you* can produce one? Presumably the Herodians were more likely to have one readily to hand, whereas the Pharisees probably looked on with disapproval. Perhaps crowds were beginning to gather around as the tension built.

Eventually a denarius was found and shown to Jesus. He had asked for one so that he could 'look at it' (Mark 12:15), but when it arrived there is no indication he touched it. His next questions did not require him, or anybody else, to observe it in any way. Everyone knew the image it bore. Caesar! And they also knew the wording inscribed upon it, which declared his divinity, usually something like 'Caesar Augustus the divine, father of the country'.

It is at this point that a *remez* comes into play. Some translations have the word 'portrait', though 'image' or 'likeness' is more likely to take us back into the scriptures. But to which particular verse or passage?

We might think the hint was to one of the Commandments where we are told not to make any graven image (Exod. 20:4, Deut. 5:8). Or maybe to the statement later in Deuteronomy that 'Cursed is anyone who makes an idol' (Deut. 27:15; 'carves an image' in some versions). But the real echo goes further back, right to the beginning where God declares that we are made in his image and likeness (Gen. 1:26-27).

By the manner in which Jesus handles this confrontation he is able to effectively issue a challenge of his own. Whose image and inscription is on *you*? Get that right and you'll know what to do. Caesar may have stamped his image on a piece of metal, but God has done something far more valuable with his image when he placed it on you.

Now we see that the phrase about rendering takes on a deep meaning. This should more properly be translated as 'give back' not just 'give'. Will you give yourself back to God? This silenced his accusers!

Was Jesus still saying it didn't matter what you did with the coin? That may be unclear, perhaps even deliberately left ambiguous. But certainly he is saying that if you do give Caesar back his coin, don't give him your worship as well. That belongs to God, whose image you bear.

We now move on to another statement of Jesus that requires some digging back into the scriptures. Let's consider a rather enigmatic and seemingly out-of-place mention of vultures.

There the vultures will gather
(Matt. 24:28, Luke 17:37)

Matthew chapter 24 is part of a great discourse on the signs of the end of the age, which Jesus gave to his disciples while seated on the Mount of Olives. But in the middle of explaining his return, he remarks, 'Wherever there is a carcass, there the vultures will gather (Matt. 24:28). What were the disciples meant to understand by that?

This sounds a bit like a proverb, and it may have become that, but there is an obvious *remez*, at least if you know the book of Job! The actual phrase in question is found at the end of chapter 39. The *remez* is in verse 30 ('where the slain are, there it is') but this is only the climax of a longer passage that starts at verse 27.

It may seem that this is about an eagle rather than a vulture, but the Hebrew word (*nasher*) refers to any large bird of prey and can mean vulture or buzzard. The main point, anyway, is that with its amazing eyesight this bird of prey can see its next meal from a great height.

It is worth adding there is no real difference in the tenses used in the Job text (present, 'there it is') and Jesus' statement (future, 'will gather'). A proverb can be stated in the present ('a stitch in time saves nine') but its meaning relates to the future (a stitch now will save more later). So

8

Jesus could just as easily have said, 'Where the dead body is, there vultures gather.' But what exactly *is* he saying?

It is helpful at this point to consider the equivalent in Luke 17:37. It doesn't seem greatly different, just a switch of dead body for carcass. But while in Matthew this remark is part of a continuous discourse by Jesus without interruption, in Luke there has just been an interjection by the disciples in the form of a question, 'Where, Lord?' So, somehow, the vultures comment is made in response to their question.

We should also note that these vultures appear at slightly different points of Jesus' teaching in the two gospels. In Matthew, Jesus has just explained that before he returns people will exclaim, 'He's over there!' or 'No, he's right here!' (see Matt. 24:26). In Luke, the preceding verses concern those who will be taken away in judgement when the Son of Man is revealed (Luke 17:30-35), something that comes a little later in Matthew's account but which also occurs at the same time as Jesus' return (Matt. 24:36-41).

In each case the same question of 'where?' can apply. Where will they go to be judged? Where will Jesus first appear on his return? In fact it seems a rather general question, simply asking for more information about what is overall a rather perplexing and complex set of interrelated events. Into this setting Jesus decides to quote this part of Job in order to give an appropriate response – 'Don't ask'!

Jesus uses this rather cryptic vulture remark at this point to tell them that he's not giving out any more details. Why? Because they don't need to know! When that moment arrives everything will happen automatically, instinctively, miraculously. You don't need to work it out in advance, nor will you have to think about it at the time. Vultures see a dead body and there they gather. So don't be concerned about where to go or what happens to others. You will find me. In fact, I will find you. Everything will work out.

Jesus is countering both a natural sense of worry and an excess of curiosity. Vultures manage instinctively. It's the same message here. So, no more questions! What I have said is enough. And that's a good lesson for us too! When it comes to our desire to know more about his return, instead of speculating further on how, where, what, when and so on, then remember the vultures!

The finger of God
(Luke 11:20)

Our next example is found in Luke 11:20 where Jesus refers to driving out demons by 'the finger of God'. In Matthew we find the equivalent statement but with the phrase 'by the Spirit of God' instead (Matt. 12:28). So we at least know what this anthropomorphism means: finger represents the Spirit. But is there a *remez* here as well?

We might assume this is intended to lead us back to the Ten Commandments, which were inscribed on tablets of stone by the finger of God (Exod. 31:18, Deut. 9:10). But the passage in the gospels is not about the Law at all. Incidentally, when Jesus was challenged to make a decision concerning a woman caught in adultery, he wrote on the ground with his finger rather than speak (John 8:2-8). This may well have been an intentional non-verbal *remez* back to the giving of the Law as this situation involving adultery *was* a legal matter (John 8:5). I'll leave you to work that one through!

Meanwhile, back to Luke 11:20, which is a demonstration of the power of God in the working of miracles. The particular *remez* is to Exodus 8:19, where the magicians of Pharaoh were unable to reproduce by their secret arts the miracles that Moses and Aaron performed. Their conclusion was, 'This is the finger of God.'

Initially, the magicians could duplicate the feats of Moses and Aaron, but in the end they were beaten. The confession that this was 'the finger of God' was intended to convey that Moses and Aaron were not simply magicians pulling off clever tricks. Indeed, they possessed no power in themselves, no magic arts. This was God at work.

The miracle in Luke chapter 11 involved healing a man who was mute through demon possession (in Matthew's account he was also blind, Matt. 12:22). This was a miracle which no-one had been able to perform, until Jesus. Here was the finger of God at work as in the past with Moses, so the outcome should have been to welcome Jesus as Messiah and herald of the kingdom of God. But, like Pharaoh, hearts were hardened instead and Jesus was rejected. Would the consequences for the religious leaders be the same?

Living water
(John 7:38)

Another simple *remez* occurs in John 7:38 where Jesus declares that anyone who believes in him will experience 'rivers of living water' flowing from him. Again, we are soon told what this means – the Spirit of God, which all believers were later to receive (John 7:39).

It is significant that Jesus proclaimed this loudly in public on the last day of the Feast of Tabernacles, when the water offering was traditionally drawn from the pool of Siloam and poured out on the altar in the Temple (something else for you to work through!). But there is another reference to consider, found in Jeremiah 2:13. 'My people have committed two sins: They have forsaken me, the spring of living water, and have dug their own cisterns, broken cisterns that cannot hold water.'

Living water was a common expression for water which flowed, such as a spring, and in spiritual terms depicted a living relationship with God. By contrast, water in a cistern was still and potentially stale, and referred to living by a man-made system of rules and regulations. This water might sustain a few people for a while but could easily stagnate. Certainly it couldn't spread life to others.

As Psalm 1:3 indicates, for a tree to be fruitful, and hence beneficial for others, it must be planted by streams of water. Being in continual touch with the living God is the only way to 'prosper', which in Hebraic thinking means to bring goodness and well-being to others. For us, prosperity suggests being acquisitive, getting more for ourselves, but in Biblical terms it is about making others better off. The living water of the Spirit flowing from within us brings blessing to all we come in contact with.

A ladder to heaven
(John 1:51)

Let's look at one final *remez* from Jesus, spoken to Nathanael while he sat under a fig tree, presumably resting in the shade in the middle of a hot day. Jesus told him he would see heaven open, and the angels of God ascending and descending on the Son of Man (John 1:51).

This is an obvious reference to Jacob's experience when he dreamt of a ladder resting on the earth but reaching up to heaven with angels ascending and descending on it (Gen. 28:12). This is not a Messianic prophecy but Jesus used it to hint that he is that ladder, the means of mediation and communication between heaven and earth, between God and Man. This clearly impressed Nathanael who became a disciple on the spot.

The Father gave hints too!
(Mark 1:11, 9:7)

We end this chapter by noticing that God the Father also dropped hints of this kind when speaking about Jesus. At his baptism a voice from heaven declared, 'You are my Son, whom I love; with you I am well pleased' (Mark 1:11). All three parts of this come from the scriptures: Psalm 2:7, Genesis 22:2, Isaiah 42:1. See what you make of these!

Later, at the transfiguration, something identical occurs (Mark 9:7). At least the first two parts are the same, while the third is now a hint to a promise to raise up another prophet like Moses (Deut. 18:15). You must listen to him!

Listening to the Jewish Jesus is precisely what we are doing!

PART FOUR

Other Puzzling Passages

Chapter Twenty

A Distressing Baptism

Luke 12:50

In these next few chapters we will look at more occasions when Jesus 'opened his mouth and spoke' as a Jew to Jews. Let's start with one of his more emotional statements, which also has an intriguing reference to a baptism.

'I have a baptism to undergo and what constraint I am under until it is completed!' (Luke 12:50)

There are several translational issues in the verse. Many other options have been offered for 'constraint'. For instance, 'what stress I am under' or 'how distressed I am'. 'Distressed' is also rendered 'pressed' or 'pained'. Certainly there is strong emotion involved, but how does this relate to baptism? What is this baptism, anyway?

Clearly not his water baptism, as this had already happened and was hardly a distressing experience for Jesus. One common view is that this baptism refers to his forthcoming suffering and death on the cross. Certainly this would match Mark 10:38-39, where baptism is linked with drinking the cup, a reference to suffering and martyrdom.

However, in Luke 12:50, this interpretation doesn't seem to fit the context. Here, this enigmatic remark is coupled with another equally mystifying comment in the preceding verse.

'I have come to bring fire on the earth, and how I wish it were already kindled!' (Luke 12:49)

By looking at these two verses together the meaning starts to emerge as they act in parallel, which means they say something similar in slightly different words, so each helps interpret the other. So what does verse 49 tell us?

We have already seen in an earlier chapter that the phrase 'I have come' is a Hebraic way of denoting intention or purpose. It is a mission statement rather than a declaration of his incarnation or any particular journey. As such it can relate to something in the future rather than an immediate task. It is part of an overall assignment that one day will be completed. With this understanding we would expect the phrase 'I have come' to be followed by an infinitive, a verb of intent, which is the case here, namely, 'to bring fire'.

In verse 49 there also is a strong sense of emotion, an intense feeling of yearning expressed in the phrase 'how I wish'. This matches the distress mentioned in the following verse.

But the main point of consideration is still about this baptism and, in particular, whether it is something that Jesus will do (active) or something that will be done to him (passive). The Hebrew word (*tovel*) behind the Greek *baptizo* can be active or passive depending on context (also called transitive or intransitive). In the Greek, and hence the English, it is the latter, but in Hebrew it could also be the former, and because of the parallelism with the preceding verse (I have come to do something) this is the most likely option. In which case we should have 'I have a baptism to *undertake*' not *undergo*.

So if this is something Jesus must do or administer, rather than something that will happen to him, he cannot be referring to any forthcoming suffering he will go through, either in Gethsemane or at the hands of the Romans, or even at Calvary. Admittedly, a similar emotional response would make sense for any of these (see Mark 14:33, for instance), together with a longing to get it over with, but this is not the context in this case. Here we have Jesus with a task to complete, a mission to fulfil, and he will not be completely at ease until he has carried it through. So what is this undertaking?

To help with this we need to look back at something John the Baptist said just before Jesus was baptised. Speaking to the religious leaders who had gathered around him, John declared that Jesus would baptise 'with the Holy Spirit and fire' (Matt. 3:11). This refers to two distinct actions, which should not be confused. Although at Pentecost 'They saw what seemed to be tongues of fire that separated and came to rest on each of them' (Acts 2:3), this is not the fire that John was speaking about. For John, fire meant judgement.

There are two images associated with John's message in this passage. One is the axe already at the root of the trees that are not producing good fruit. The other is the winnowing fork, an implement similar to a pitchfork but with larger blades, used to separate the grain from the chaff. Initially the wheat is threshed while still on the floor by the operation of a threshing board being pulled across it, usually by a donkey. This starts the process of separation. Then the winnowing fork tosses it all in the air where the chaff is blown away by the breeze, which is technically when the winnowing takes place.

In both illustrations there is a final reference to the fire of judgement and destruction. The bad trees are 'thrown into the fire' (Matt. 3:10), and the chaff will be burned up 'with unquenchable fire' (Matt. 3:12). So to be consistent, the mention of 'fire' in verse 11 must also provide the same picture, and it is this 'baptism of fire', or of judgement, which stands in contrast to baptism in the Holy Spirit.

So now our verses in Luke chapter 12 make sense both separately and as a pair. Jesus will one day baptise the earth with fire. When he returns, he will bring judgement and destruction, and it is this that he is not looking forward to. It distresses him to think of this part of his mission and he wishes he could get it over with as soon as possible.

Verse 49 has the word 'kindled', which suggests a fire just starting. In Hebrew 'burn' has a wide range of meanings. Two can be found in Exodus 3:2, where the bush was 'on fire' (it had broken out in flames, it was burning) but it did not 'burn up' (it was not consumed). It seems that in verse 49 Jesus is wishing that the final judgement had already started, and in verse 50 he is indicating the distress he will feel until it is all over and the earth has been completely consumed.

As we said above, context is important, which is why we connected verses 49 and 50. But we should also look at the few verses that follow. Notice they also start with 'I have come'. Our translation may have 'I came' but this is just an English variation. Hebrew has just one past tense whereas we have many, so there is no real difference in meaning. Jesus is again thinking of his mission and how it is already bringing division. This will continue until the very end. 'From now on' (verse 52) families will be split. Some people will be for him, others will be against him, and hence against others in the same family.

Verses 51 to 53 help us to understand Jesus' statements in the two preceding verses. Also that the delay, necessary to allow for more to turn to God in repentance and faith, is both an ongoing sign of God's mercy but also a source of distress for Jesus as he watches all this division unfold.

It might be helpful to attempt a paraphrase of this section to bring out all the meaning we have uncovered.

'My task is to set the earth on fire and I am already doing this. The seeds of judgement are being sown even now as families divide over me, and one day, on my return, there will be a final destruction, which I am not looking forward to. As part of the mission I have been given, I am required to immerse the earth in judgement, and it fills me with distress right now as I see some rejecting me and my claims, and so storing up judgement for themselves.'

One final point should be made. Do we share these emotions of Jesus? We may be looking ahead with joy to our Saviour's return and all that will mean for us in terms of a blissful future, but what about those who have rejected him? Are we as distressed as Jesus about their fate? If not, then we should keep these verses before us as a constant reminder of the full impact of his return to earth.

Chapter Twenty-One

Who's Afraid of the Big Bad Fox?

Luke 13:32

In Luke 13:32, Jesus called Herod Antipas a 'fox'. Why did he do this? And what exactly did he mean?

When we describe someone as a fox we are influenced by proverbs and fables which tell us that foxes are cunning and crafty, even sly. 'Fox' does have this same connotation in Greek and sometimes also in Hebrew, but by Jesus' time it had a wider range of meanings. It had become a cultural metaphor, which is what Jesus drew on here.

Let's first of all see the full context of this designation of Herod as a fox before we consider why Jesus chose that particular epithet and what he was saying about Herod's character.

> 'At that time some Pharisees came to Jesus and said to him, "Leave this place and go somewhere else. Herod wants to kill you." He replied, "Go and tell that fox, 'I will keep on driving out demons and healing people today and tomorrow, and on the third day I will reach my goal.' In any case, I must press on today and tomorrow and the next day – for surely no prophet can die outside Jerusalem!"' (Luke 13:31-33)

In these few verses Jesus is being warned of danger and told that he should flee for his life. Note that it is *some* of the Pharisees who alerted him, showing that not all Pharisees were hostile to Jesus. Indeed in the next chapter of Luke we find Jesus enjoying hospitality in the house of a prominent Pharisee.

The Herod mentioned was Herod Antipater (or Antipas), one of the sons of Herod the Great. Some background here is both important and useful. It is easy to get muddled when it comes to Herod's family!

There are three sons of Herod the Great mentioned in the gospels. Two of them, Archelaus and Antipas, were full brothers. Their mother was Malthace, a Samaritan woman. As Herod the Great was an Idumaean, these two brothers were half Idumaean and half Samaritan. The other son, Philip, also called Herod Philip II, was a half-brother of Archelaus and Antipas, as his mother was Cleopatra of Jerusalem, Herod the Great's fifth wife.

On the death of Herod the Great, his kingdom was divided between these three sons. Archelaus, being the oldest (though only eighteen at the time), inherited the largest portion (about half), namely Judea, Samaria and Idumea (Edom). He was given the title of 'ethnarch', which is lower than that of a king, and simply means leader or governor of people.

Antipas inherited the province of Galilee and also Perea on the eastern side of the River Jordan. He ruled these areas from 4 BC to AD 39, which coincided with most of Jesus' life and all of his ministry. As this territory constituted roughly a quarter of his father's kingdom, Antipas was known as a 'tetrarch', or 'ruler of a fourth' (Matt. 14:1).

His half-brother, Philip, also ruled as a tetrarch. Philip took over the north-eastern portion of his father's kingdom, the territories of Ituraea and Trachonitis, which he ruled from 4 BC to AD 34.

A map of this territorial division between the sons of Herod is a useful aid to Bible study. It enables us to see who was in charge of the different regions in which Jesus ministered and explains why he sometimes moved on. For instance, by crossing the Sea of Galilee he would be switching between the tetrarchies of Antipas and Philip.

However, for reasons explained later in this chapter, Archelaus only ruled from 4 BC to AD 6, when he was replaced by a Roman Governor named Pontius Pilate. So Archelaus was not in power during the time of Jesus' ministry and had no influence upon him during those years. But Archelaus did play a key part in the *early* life of Jesus. Archelaus was particularly violent and barbaric (more on this later), and it was this tyranny that determined where Jesus would be brought up.

Joseph, Mary and the young Jesus had fled to Egypt to escape the murderous wrath of Herod the Great. When Herod died it seemed safe for them to return to the land of Israel, but when Joseph heard that Archelaus was not much better than his father and that he was in charge of Judea, Joseph decided they should settle in Nazareth in Galilee (where Antipas ruled) rather than go back to Bethlehem in Judea (see Matt. 2:19-23).

Galilee was a particularly significant area for Jesus' ministry, so he was in the territory of Herod Antipas a large amount of the time. It was also Antipas who had been rebuked by

John the Baptist for various sins and so he imprisoned John (Luke 3:19-20) and eventually had him beheaded.

Returning to Luke 13:31-33, we may not be sure exactly what had caused Herod Antipas to get angry with Jesus and seek to kill him, but despite this threat Jesus did not flee. Rather, he stated that he would do the opposite and continue with his mission until he had brought it to completion, which involved going to Jerusalem. It is in this context that he describes Herod as a fox. So what did this mean?

In first-century Jewish culture, calling someone a fox was intended to contrast him with a lion. Great men were called lions; lesser men were called foxes. Comparisons of this kind were also made regarding intelligence. 'Lions' were those renowned for their intellectual ability; 'foxes' less so. For instance, of someone thought to be brilliant but who proved to be inept it might be said, 'The lion turns out to be a mere fox.' In another case, you might show humility by saying, 'There are lions before you and you ask a fox?' meaning, 'Why ask me when there are others here much cleverer?'

The lion-fox analogy was also used of pedigree. 'He is a lion, the son of a lion' was an accolade for someone who lived up to his eminent parentage. 'He is a lion, the son of a fox' could also be a compliment as it suggested someone had risen above his natural origins. You can guess what 'he's a fox, the son of a fox' was meant to imply!

In addition, a Jewish proverb stated, 'It is better to be a tail to lions than a head to foxes', indicating that a lesser role among prominent people is more beneficial than being a leader among fools! You will learn more, and grow morally stronger, if you associate yourself, however lowly, with those of greater calibre.

So now we see that when Jesus referred to Herod as a fox, he was not making any kind of positive comment, not even that Herod had certain qualities of cunning which meant he ruled well. He was no lion. At best he was a fox, the son of a lion, but not in any way did he live up to the celebrated fame and impressive talent of his father, Herod, called 'Great'. Antipas might consider himself to be of equal stature and reputation, but Jesus did not think of him this way, and so he was not afraid. Antipas was no real threat, so Jesus would be able to continue his mission and reach his goal.

By his choice of words Jesus cut Herod down to size. 'Someone like him doesn't worry me!' Of course, Jesus also knew that he was fulfilling his Father's will and that nothing could stop this now. He was on his way to Jerusalem for the final time, to be 'delivered into the hands of men' (Luke 9:44) and then 'to be taken up into heaven' (Luke 9:51; we will examine this verse more in a later chapter). So Herod could not prevent God's purpose anyway, but the fox reference was a neat way of making this point, and one which may have brought a smile to the faces of those who were listening to Jesus.

What word might we use today instead of 'fox' to make a similar statement? Weakling, maybe, or small-fry? A mere nobody? Perhaps if this was someone in a position of authority whom we regarded as effectively powerless, we might choose usurper or pretender.

There is one final point worth making which relates to the rule of Antipas and also his brother Archelaus. In Luke 19:12, Jesus begins to tell the people a parable, that of the ten minas, which is similar to the better-known parable of the talents (Matt. 25:14-30). However, instead of a man going on a journey, Luke's account is more specific: 'A man of noble birth went to a distant country to have himself appointed king and then to return' (Luke 19:12). This provides the parable with a setting based upon a real-life event. This would immediately register with Jesus' listeners. For us, this means another history lesson!

When Herod the Great died, his three sons had to travel to Rome to get permission to rule. Even though their father had granted this in his will, it was not automatic. The emperor, Augustus, had to agree to this, perhaps aided by a small (or not so small!) 'gift'.

Apparently, Herod had changed his will a few days before his death, making Archelaus his main heir instead of Antipas. No doubt this made the journey to Rome rather more strained than it might otherwise have been! When Archelaus argued his case against the claims of his brothers, Augustus sided with him and confirmed him in possession of the largest portion. But, as we said earlier, the emperor did not make him king, but gave him the lesser title of 'ethnarch' instead, effectively putting him on probation. After all, he was just eighteen years old! Perhaps the idea was that he would be promoted to king if he proved himself an able ruler.

But Archelaus proved to be the very opposite. Soon after returning to Jerusalem his crowd control at Passover went badly wrong and his soldiers massacred three thousand

Jews in and around the Temple. After more atrocities he was eventually deposed in AD 6 and his territory became a Roman province under the authority of a Roman governor, namely Pontius Pilate. Meanwhile, Archelaus was exiled to Gaul where he died in AD 18, by which time, as we have seen, Joseph, Mary and Jesus had gone to live in Nazareth (Matt. 2:19-23).

So we find that the opening of Jesus' parable in Luke chapter 19 had a strong parallel in history: a noble man (or in this case men) go to a distant country to get power. A knowing smile would have spread across the faces of those listening.

Moreover, the similarities didn't end there. In Luke 19:14-15 we read, 'But his subjects hated him and sent a delegation after him to say, "We don't want this man to be our king." He was made king, however, and returned home.'

In the real-life event, a delegation of Jews soon followed the sons of Herod to Rome to petition Augustus. They listed a long catalogue of crimes which Herod the Great had committed against the Jewish people and begged the emperor not to allow his sons to have power over them. They would rather have the Romans rule them directly than more Herods! However, Augustus dismissed their arguments and maintained his appointment of Antipas and Archelaus as tetrarch and ethnarch, respectively. Archelaus' response to the Jewish attempt to deny him power was to hunt down and kill members of the delegation and their families. His reign of terror continued for several years until, finally, the emperor lost patience and deposed him.

This piece of history interacts strongly with what Jesus was saying in both Luke chapter 13 and chapter 19. Although Archelaus was no longer in power in Judea, Antipas still held sway in the Galilee. But he was more of a puppet ruler than a sovereign by his own authority or even by popular consensus. Rome retained the real power. Herod was no more than a big, bad fox. Jesus knew he was not going to die at Herod's hands, so why fear his threats?

Chapter Twenty-Two

Telling the Truth

Reading through the gospels it is remarkable how often we find Jesus saying, 'I tell you the truth', or its equivalent. By some counts this is over seventy times, though this includes double and treble accounting when the phrase occurs in parallel passages across more than one gospel. Why did Jesus say this so much? Does it imply that on other occasions he wasn't always as truthful?

We might say 'I'm telling you the truth' in an attempt to boost our credibility or convince a sceptical listener, but we would hesitate to suggest this was necessary for Jesus. Instead we might suspect there is something Hebraic behind these statements – and we would be right! Jesus was employing not only a common idiomatic saying but, as part of this, a very familiar Hebrew word, one we all use: 'Amen!'

We have become so accustomed to tacking this word onto the end of a prayer that we probably never give it much thought. We might have been taught that it is a devout way of saying 'so be it' or be vaguely aware that we are expressing agreement in some appropriately pious way. In fact, it is a regular word in Hebrew that covers a variety of meanings such as 'firm', 'established', 'true', or even 'sure!'

Our word 'amen' is simply the four letters of the Hebrew word turned into their English equivalents. This is called transliteration, which means the word has not been translated into a known English word, rather a new word has been created from the Hebrew letters and added to our language.

The same happened in Greek and so in the gospels we also find 'amen' made up of the four Greek letters which match those in Hebrew. So we get *'amen lego umin'*, which in older English versions was rendered as 'truly I say unto you' or even 'verily I say unto you'. In addition, it is noticeable that in every such reference in John's Gospel the *'amen'* is repeated, which explains why we have 'truly, truly [verily, verily] I say unto you', or even 'very truly I tell you'. Why this is peculiar to one gospel is uncertain, but this doubling emphasises even more the Hebraic nature of the statement.

Also worth noting is that in this phrase 'you' is nearly always plural, but it can be singular, for instance when Jesus is addressing Peter (Matt. 26:34), in which case the Greek text has *'amen lego soi'*. Another occasion would be when Jesus is debating with Nicodemus (John 3:3) where, as it is in John's Gospel, the Greek has the doubled form, *'amen amen lego soi'*.

Moreover, there are also examples of *'lego gar umin'* (for I say unto you) without the *'amen'*, and cases of *'amen lego gar umin'*, which would be rendered in modern versions as 'For I tell you the truth'. But what should be noted here is that the *'amen'*, whenever it does occur, is always at the beginning of the phrase.

And that's the main point – the position of 'Amen!' In the English phrase it has been turned round and placed at the end, '[For] I tell you the truth'. Instead it should be 'True! I say to you ...'

This indicates that the *'amen'* is affirming what has just been said or something that has just happened. It is not qualifying what is about to be said. This is how we use the word at the end of a prayer, agreeing with what has just been prayed rather than anything to follow. We are endorsing the prayer by adding our own 'That's right!'

Also, in the case of the full Hebraic phrase 'Amen, I say to you', the second part (after 'amen') is a typical rabbinic way of continuing what has just been upheld, and acts as a sort of 'furthermore'. When someone says this he is not only supporting the previous statement or action but emphasising its significance by adding something himself, perhaps seeking to develop the point further. Effectively, he is responding by saying, 'Here is something so true that it is worthy of additional comment.'

So we should realise that when Jesus says, 'I tell you the truth', his use of 'truth' (*amen*) is not to qualify what he is about to say as though otherwise he might not be telling the whole truth and nothing but the truth. Rather, he is indicating something along the lines of 'I agree with this, but there's more to add so listen to what I now have to say'.

As we might expect, this phrase also occurs in the Old Testament; even an angel says this on one occasion (Dan. 11:2)! But it is in the gospels that we come across it much more, though only in the mouth of Jesus where it is a regular feature. In this chapter we will have a brief look at a selection of these; edited highlights, you might say. If you want to check them all out, the full list is in Appendix B.

Bear in mind that in all of these occurrences we are looking for an endorsement of something preceding. This might be either something just said or something just done. And it may be by someone else or even by the speaker himself. It was quite normal in rabbinic practice to agree with yourself for effect before continuing what you are wanting to get across!

We start in Mark 12:41-43, where Jesus endorses what someone has done and then draws a lesson from it. Jesus is sitting in the Temple area, with his disciples nearby, watching people put their offerings into the collection boxes. We have commented on this in an earlier chapter when discussing 'sounding the trumpet'. Now we notice that Jesus calls his disciples to him and begins to teach them by saying, 'I tell you the truth'. His 'Amen to that' is directed towards the action of the poor widow and her offering. Effectively, Jesus is saying: 'Look at that! That's true giving', and then he makes a further comment on what is right about this particular example of truth in action. Here is a typically rabbinic mode of teaching, both in how it starts and in the drawing of a conclusion from seeing what someone has done.

Our next example is in Mark 14:3-9, where Jesus is a guest at the home of Simon the Leper. The meal is interrupted by a woman pouring a jar of expensive perfume over Jesus' head. Some of those present complain at the waste, but Jesus affirms what has just taken place. In particular, he declares she has performed an action that represents preparing him for burial, which will happen very soon.

'Amen! She's right to do this!' His additional comment is that her deed will be remembered forever as part of the gospel account.

In the Gospel of Matthew there are several more occasions when this phrase played an important role in situations where Jesus delivered some of his main teachings.

In Matthew 8:10, the words and faith of a centurion so astonished Jesus that he declares a mighty 'Amen!' 'Just listen to that!' he seems to be saying, and follows up what the centurion has said with teaching on how faith like this will bring many Gentiles into the kingdom at the expense of unbelieving Jews (Matt. 8:5-13).

At the start of Matthew chapter 18 Jesus faces a question from his disciples about who is greatest in the kingdom of heaven. He responds by placing a small child in their midst, then reinforces his own actions with an 'amen' (Matt. 18:3). 'That's right! This is what It's all about. Now learn from this.'

A further example is in Matthew 19:23. When the rich young man was challenged by Jesus to sell all he had and give to the poor, he went away sad because he had great wealth. Jesus used an 'amen' to draw attention to what had just happened. As with the widow's offering, this was intended to alert his disciples to someone else's action. 'Take note of what you see here, and understand from this how dangerous riches can be' (Matt. 19:16-24).

Then there is Matthew 21:28-31. In the parable of the two sons Jesus asked those listening to him which of the sons did what his father wanted. 'The first', they answered. Jesus' response was, 'Amen! Exactly! You've got it, so now here's more to think about.'

Before we end this chapter we should see how Jesus used this phrase in the course of a discussion with another rabbi. In John chapter 3 we read of the famous meeting between Jesus and Nicodemus who came to see Jesus after nightfall. Much is often made of the fact that he came 'at night', as though it had to be in secret or that he was embarrassed to be seen visiting Jesus. This is pure speculation. Nicodemus had probably arranged to visit in the evening as this was when rabbis usually met. They often had a daytime job as well. It may also be so he could bring some of his own disciples as well. This would account for the 'we' in his opening remarks (John 3:2), though he may simply have been making a rather grandiose statement about himself! But a rabbi would usually have his disciples with him when meeting another rabbi. Presumably Jesus had some of his disciples there too. It seems likely John was present.

Whatever the reason for the timing of the visit, Nicodemus began, rather politely, by explaining how they all recognised Jesus as 'a teacher who has come from God' and why this was so apparent to them (John 3:2). We have mentioned this before when considering the matter of the authority that Jesus showed, but now we are more interested in how Jesus begins his reply. By starting with 'I tell you the truth' (John 3:3), which, if you recall, is always in 'double form' in John's Gospel ('amen, amen, I say unto you'), Jesus is affirming what Nicodemus has just stated about him. 'Yes, Nicodemus, you're right! I *am* from God. My miracles *do* show this. And God *is* with me. So what I'm going to say next about a new birth is very important, however difficult it might seem to you at first.'

Then, when Nicodemus responds incredulously with a rhetorical question about the impossibility of being physically born a second time, Jesus uses the phrase once more (John 3:5). 'You're right again, Nicodemus! Of course it's impossible. So let's discuss this further.'

As a slight aside it is worth noting that Jesus talks about being 'born again', or 'born from above', with Nicodemus but not with anyone else, for instance the Samaritan woman in the next chapter of John. If it is so essential ('You must be born again', John 3:7), why was it not always part of Jesus' evangelism?

The answer is because it made the point particularly well to an educated middle-aged Jewish man such as Nicodemus. This was not a new phrase invented by Jesus. It was already in use in various ways. Nicodemus would have been familiar with the term within the context of his physical life as it was used to refer to big life-changing events such as getting married, joining the Sanhedrin or becoming 'Israel's teacher'. In his own mind Nicodemus had already been 'born again' as often as possible, which is why he questions how a man can be born *when he is old* (John 3:4, italics mine). At his age he was too old for any more 'new births' such as these, hence he makes what appears to be something of a jest. After all, repeating your physical birth is not age-dependent. It does not matter how much time has elapsed; a second physical birth is not possible even one minute afterwards.

We see another 'amen' phrase in John 3:11 and it is likely Jesus continued in this vein throughout the dialogue. It was such a common feature in rabbinic discussion and the two Jewish teachers surely talked together for much longer that the gospel records. Only a brief account is given for us by John. Likewise our survey of this Hebraic idiom has been limited by space, but the full list of references is in Appendix B if you want to explore further.

Chapter Twenty-Three

Swords and Ears

Luke 22:47-51, John 15:1, Luke 9:44

The arrest of Jesus
(Luke 22:47-51)

All four gospels relate the arrest of Jesus, which is not surprising, but as part of this event each gives a slightly different report of a strange incident involving a flashing sword and a mutilated right ear.

'Lord, should we strike with our swords?' the disciples ask. And seemingly before an answer can be given, a blade swishes and an unfortunate young man suddenly has only half the number of ears he woke up with that morning (Luke 22:49-50). We learn elsewhere that it was Peter who struck the blow and that the hapless recipient was called Malchus, one of the servants of the high priest (John 18:10).

A less gruesome ending is provided by Luke who, perhaps because he was a doctor, wants us to know that Jesus 'touched the man's ear and healed him' (Luke 22:51). We are also told that Jesus then rebuked his disciples (presumably mainly Peter) for this assault, a reprimand which includes the well-known words 'all who draw the sword will die by the sword' (Matt. 26:52; also Luke 22:51, John 18:11).

Piecing together these four accounts provides a clear picture of the event, but still leaves certain questions to be considered. Why were they carrying swords? How many did they have? Why attack an ear? Perhaps this was Peter's aim, literally, or maybe he intended something far worse but in the gloom of the Gethsemane garden only managed a glancing blow. By looking more closely into the whole affair we may also learn why Jesus healed Malchus, other than out of pure compassion, and to stop the screaming!

For answers to all these questions we should start by going back earlier in the day and join Jesus and his disciples at their Passover meal. 'When the hour came, Jesus and his apostles reclined at the table' (Luke 22:14). This was not any kind of table around which we would normally sit. Rather, it was a triclinium, a set of three couches surrounding a low serving table and upon which guests would recline on their left side. Before taking up this position, sandals would be removed and feet washed, a necessary procedure given the proximity of your feet to the person reclining next to you.

But reclining in such a way meant that you, and indeed the whole party, were vulnerable to attack should anyone with evil intent decide to gate-crash your meal. So those who occupied the two ends of the U-shaped triclinium acted as bodyguards, or defenders, should it prove necessary. Each would have a sword on their person, or at least nearby, as wearing a sword while reclining could do more harm than any intruder, either to yourself or fellow diners. But with swords close to hand, those at the ends of the table could jump up, grab a sword and quickly provide some kind of protection or resistance.

That explains the comment made by the disciples, 'See, Lord, here are two swords' (Luke 22:38). It also helps us understand the meaning behind Jesus' reply, 'That is enough.' We might easily read this as 'That'll do', in the sense of 'Be quiet! Don't talk like that!' implying that they should leave the swords alone and forget about them. Instead it is more likely that Jesus was saying that two would be sufficient for now and they needn't go looking for more.

Moreover, Jesus had just told them that now would be a good time to buy a sword if they didn't already have one (Luke 22:36). If necessary they should sell their cloak, a vital outer garment which we discussed in an earlier chapter. They may not have needed a sword in the past, but the situation had changed and become more dangerous. Previously they had been sent out without any provisions at all (Luke 22:35, see Matt. 10:9-10), but then it was much safer to be a follower of Jesus. Now Jesus knew he was about to be arrested, and those coming for him would have clubs and swords of their own. He wanted his disciples to feel they could defend themselves if necessary. However, as we have already seen, he wasn't asking them to take swords to attack those who were arresting him. He could have called on twelve legions of angels (Matt. 26:53), so he didn't need their help!

It is worth considering at this point what type of sword this would have been. The Greek, *machaira*, can cover a variety of weapons but in this case it most likely refers to something akin to a dagger. It would certainly have been a short sword, one-edged and curved, primarily designed to cut rather than thrust. In contrast to the larger swords carried by Roman soldiers, the *machaira* was a more domestic implement, often used for killing animals and cutting up the flesh. It could also be a useful instrument for exacting retribution!

So off they went, Jesus and his disciples, two swords at hand, one of them more specifically in the hand of Peter. Perhaps Peter had been one of those at the ends of the table, or perhaps he just took charge as usual. 'I'll take that now!' Either way, he struck the blow. So far, all this explains the swords, but what about the ear?

It is likely that when Peter wielded the sword he knew exactly what he was doing, and to whom. This was no fluke but a deliberate aim. And it was not just any random mobster that Peter attacked. This was one of the servants of the high priest, perhaps even his chief assistant, the one supervising the arrest. Killing him would be real trouble! But maiming him in this way would lead to quite different consequences.

According to Jewish Law, losing an ear would disqualify someone from serving in the Temple as no-one with a blemish or defect of any kind could enter the holy place (Lev. 21:18-21). In fact, in Jewish history one way of preventing someone from holding an official position in the Temple was to cut off an ear lobe. So it is possible Peter was aiming to do this, a sufficient punishment in his mind. And maybe that is one reason why Jesus restored the ear, though all this may be reading too much into a spur-of-the-moment occurrence.

The Golden Vine
(John 15:1)

Putting ears to one side for a moment, let's fill in a small but engaging detail that transpired on the way from the room of the Last Supper to Gethsemane. The shortest route would have taken them through the Temple courts, which would still have been open in the evening at this time of the year. As part of their journey, Jesus and his disciples would have walked past the Temple itself, where a man-made golden vine was wrapped around the columns at the entrance to the sanctuary.

This Golden Vine was magnificent and famous enough to get a mention by Tacitus in his Histories (History 5.5). Another historian, Josephus, records that its size, artistry and costly materials made it a marvel of its time. Its branches were 'hanging down from a great height, the largeness and fine workmanship of which was a surprising sight to the spectators to see what vast materials there were, and with what great skill the workmanship was done' (Antiquities, Book 15, 11:3). It is reckoned that some of the grapes were the height of a man.

Moreover, anyone wealthy enough could purchase a golden leaf or grape, or if very wealthy then a cluster, which the priests would attach to the vine. Such generosity was rewarded by having your name inscribed on one of the leaves. This was a custom that everyone in Jerusalem at the time was familiar with.

Why is this relevant to our theme? Because once again we see our Jewish rabbi taking advantage of a situation to bring some important teaching about himself. This was the last time Jesus would be with all his disciples before his arrest. This was his final walk through Jerusalem with them. He wanted to give them something they would remember, so it was while walking past this artificial vine that Jesus said, 'I am the true vine' (John 15:1).

The very end of John chapter 14 continues a small detail that is often missed: 'Come now; let us leave' (John 14:31). This shows they now leave the Passover room and make their way towards Gethsemane. Moreover, it is not until John 18:1 that they cross the Kidron valley and enter the garden of Gethsemane. So all of Jesus' teaching in John chapters 15 and 16, plus his famous prayer in chapter 17, takes place while on this walk through Jerusalem, or perhaps while they had paused near the Temple to gaze at the Golden Vine.

Jesus is the true vine, far more valuable or real than anything golden or man-made. And we can be branches of the true vine. If we attach ourselves to him and remain in him then we will bear real fruit. Every time in the future his disciples went to the Temple and saw this artificial vine they would recall these words and all he meant by them.

Listen carefully
(Luke 9:44)

Before we leave this chapter, we have another ear-based statement to comment upon. In Luke 9:44 we read, 'Listen carefully to what I am about to tell you.' This is a good translation of a fascinating Hebrew idiom, which is no doubt what Jesus actually used.

For this verse the Authorised Version has 'Let these sayings sink down into your ears', which is based upon a literal translation of the Greek, so it is accurate if somewhat archaic, as is the wonderfully expressive 'Lay these sayings in your ears'. This delightful turn of phrase fully conveys the message of 'listen very carefully . . .' but isn't one we would normally use. Imagine your teacher saying this to you!

So why was it chosen by Jesus here? Perhaps because of its use within his scriptures, in particular in Exodus 17:14. The background is the defeat of the Amalekites achieved largely by Joshua but also thanks to an epic daylong hand-raising effort by Moses, supported (literally) towards the end by Aaron and Hur.

After this notable victory the Lord told Moses to record the events on a scroll 'as something to be remembered' or, more literally, as a memorial. God then added that Moses was also to 'make sure that Joshua hears it' (Exod. 17:14). The Hebrew is the more graphic 'Place it in the ears of Joshua', which gives rise to the idiom Jesus used.

The implication of the phrase was clear. Joshua had to *really* take note of this. These were not just to be words on a scroll, occasionally read and easily forgotten. Joshua had to hear these words and retain them. This could not be a case of 'in one ear and out the other'; he had to lay these words in his ears so that they really sank in and stayed there.

The reason is given in the remaining verses (Exod. 17:15-16). The Amalekites were going to be a constant enemy of Israel. There would be many more battles from this point on but one day the Amalekites would be utterly destroyed by the Lord and their memory blotted out. Meanwhile, this initial victory was to be remembered by Israel forever. Knowing what God had done for them on this occasion and what he promised them in the future would keep them going when it was really tough. So, Joshua, lay all this firmly in your ears. You'll need it again one day!

Likewise, Jesus used this phrase because of the importance of what he was saying. These were momentous words: 'The Son of Man is going to be betrayed into the hands of men' (Luke 9:44). Jesus was now on his way to Jerusalem to be rejected and put to death. His disciples wouldn't understand what he was saying at this point. That this could happen to their Jesus was unthinkable! So Jesus reinforces his announcement with this ear-based idiomatic phrase so that his disciples would keep its message in mind for the days ahead when it would become increasingly meaningful.

Listening carefully to the Jewish Jesus provides us with insights such as these, which can really aid our Bible reading, so let's find some more!

Chapter Twenty-Four

How Near and How Wise

Matthew 4:17, 11:2-19, 24:32-33

How near is the kingdom?
(Matt. 4:17)

As we continue our quest for further Hebraic insights we will spend this chapter mainly in Matthew and the next (and final) one largely in Luke. Let's start with the first message Jesus gave as he began to preach in Galilee: 'Repent, for the kingdom of heaven is near' (Matt. 4:17).

We find a similar declaration repeated later on when Jesus sent out seventy-two of his followers as part of their discipleship training. On their travels they were to replicate the ministry of their rabbi and proclaim the same message of the nearness of the kingdom (Luke 10:9, 11). The importance of this is evident by the way Jesus insisted on them understanding this for themselves as well as passing it on to others everywhere they went.

But what exactly was Jesus hoping to convey by this statement? What does 'near' mean? And was the kingdom any nearer at that later stage than when Jesus first began preaching?

Saying that something is 'near' seems to suggest that it is nearby but not yet here. It's coming; it's on the way, but you'll have to wait a bit longer. The Greek of Matthew 4:17 can be translated 'is at hand', which is another way of saying it is within your grasp. Reach out and it's yours! This might seem a better message than the rather vague 'near', but the Hebrew equivalent is even more helpful. In Hebrew 'to come near' means to draw right up close to something, even to be at the same place. Here are some examples.

In 2 Kings 16:12, King Ahaz approached the altar, or drew near to it, and presented offerings on it. This means he went right up to it. The only way to make offerings on an altar is to be so close that there is no further distance to travel.

To approach or draw near is also used to indicate sexual relations. In Genesis 20:4 we are told that Abimelech had not gone near Sarah, Abraham's wife. This is to inform us that sexual activity had not taken place. Similarly, when Isaiah 'approached' the prophetess (presumably his wife), he went sufficiently 'near' for her to be able to conceive and give birth to a son (Isa. 8:3). Some translations actually say, 'Then I made love to the prophetess.' Then there is Deuteronomy 22:13-14, which describes how a man who has just married a woman might 'come to her' (sometimes translated as 'approached her' or 'sleep with her') and discover she was not a virgin after all. In all these cases it doesn't take much imagination to work out what kind of closeness is involved.

So in Hebraic terms, 'near' implies no distance at all, and when Jesus speaks in these terms regarding the kingdom, the same idea is intended. Although there is still a future aspect of the kingdom, it is also here for us to grasp right now. Theologians have this right when they speak of the kingdom as 'now and not yet', both realised and still to come. This is because the nature of God's kingdom is unlike earthly ones. It is not about territory but about God's rule in our lives. You can become a subject of this kingdom now by keeping God's Law and obeying his will. In this way you can 'draw near' and find the kingdom is as close as anything else you might experience.

John the Baptist has doubts
(Matt. 11:2-6)

Jesus wasn't the only one, or indeed the first, to preach that the kingdom of heaven was near. This was also the initial message of John the Baptist in the Judean desert (Matt. 3:2). But later, when In prison, it seems his conviction was somewhat shaken.

> 'When John, who was in prison, heard the deeds of the Messiah, he sent his disciples to ask him, "Are you the one who was to come or should we expect someone else?"' (Matt. 11:2-3)

Previously, John had been absolutely adamant who Jesus was. His testimony was clear: 'Look, the Lamb of God, who takes away the sin of the world ... I testify that this is God's Chosen One' (John 1:29-34). Jesus was the one who would come after him, more powerful and a baptiser in more than just water (Matt. 3:11). Now it seems John's faith was wavering. Were doubts starting to creep in now he was imprisoned?

It is likely that John was not so much questioning whether he had got it right in declaring Jesus as 'the one who was to come' (a way of describing the Messiah), rather whether *as* Messiah Jesus was doing the right things. Are you Messiah, because you aren't acting in the way I thought Messiah would? John was hearing what Christ was doing, and his deeds didn't match John's expectations. Where is the fire of judgement, the winnowing fork, the axe at the root of the trees (Matt. 3:10-12)?

It is interesting to consider what exactly John might have heard that Jesus had been doing in recent times. Without compiling a full list (an exercise for the reader!) it can perhaps be best summarised as acts of mercy rather than judgement. So John was puzzled. Jesus had preached the same message as John: the kingdom was now at hand. So why wasn't it replacing the old way of things?

Jesus replied by echoing (rather than quoting) parts of the prophets, mainly Isaiah (see, for instance, Isa. 29:18-19, 35:5-6, 61:1). There are also similarities with Psalm 146:7-8:

'He upholds the cause of the oppressed and gives food to the hungry. The Lord sets prisoners free, the Lord gives sight to the blind, the Lord lifts up those who are bowed down, the Lord loves the righteous.'

It is also of interest to note that among the Dead Sea Scrolls is a fragmentary document commonly called 'A Messianic Apocalypse' (officially categorised as 4Q521). This also outlines the earthly accomplishments of the Messiah in terms of mercy, including biblical references such as Psalm 146:7-8 and Isaiah 61:1. Was this document something John knew? And did Jesus know that John was aware of it?

Regardless of such speculation, it is clear Jesus was declaring most emphatically that this *was* the kingdom at work. But, as he went on to explain later (using the parables we studied in earlier chapters), the kingdom would start small and grow as the seeds took root. Meanwhile, there would be wheat and weeds growing together. Rather than a mighty revolution which uprooted all evil and kicked out those whose power was based upon corruption and wickedness, there was to be a steady but sure expansion of God's ways in the world.

This is the tension contained within Jesus' teaching and which the early church had to come to terms with. The kingdom being 'at hand' indicates it has already come. It has not been deferred to a later date when Jesus returns or some future judgement takes place. Jesus' reign is a present and progressing reality. But other kingdoms are also 'at hand', and have been on earth for a long time. Not just the kingdom of darkness and of Satan, but a myriad of human wills trying to run their own lives without God as their King. This clash will continue until the end of human history as we know it.

How much of this was understood by John as he languished in prison we cannot tell. We have no further response from John to what was reported back to him. Did he understand things better now? Did he accept what Jesus had said? Perhaps John had hoped for something a bit different, at least an assurance that it wouldn't be long before he was out of prison! Wasn't releasing the captives also a Messianic act?

John the Baptist as Elijah
(Matt. 11:7-15)

Once John's disciples had left, Jesus continued to address the crowds. He challenged them to think more highly of his forerunner. We have already seen in an earlier chapter how Jesus declared that John was the breach-maker, one who had enabled the kingdom to 'break through' into the world. To do this, John had needed to display toughness and resilience as a true Elijah figure, and now he was paying the price.

Jesus used the image of a reed to make his point (Matt. 11:7). When the crowds flocked to the region around the Jordan to hear John preach they would have seen many beautiful reeds. Depending on the time of day they would have seen the reeds standing tall (in the morning) or sinking down (in the heat of the afternoon) or rising up again (in the cool of the evening). They could also be observed shaking gently in the breeze. Was this somehow to depict the character of John or to describe what had happened to him?

Perhaps, but there was also a well-known parable at the time called The Reed and The Oak, which unsurprisingly is rather similar to another story called The Oak and The Reed, featured in Aesop's Fables. The contrast between the reed and the oak is shown whenever the wind blows. The reed sways in the breeze and is bent over by strong winds. The oak, meanwhile, stands firm, held by its deep roots, at least until the wind turns into a gale, at which point the oak can be toppled while the reed continues to bend, compromising more and more but able to survive the storm.

A simple mention of a reed would illustrate all that Jesus wanted to get across. 'What did you go out into the wilderness to see? A reed swayed by the wind?' (Matt. 11:7). Is this how you saw John? Or was he like a mighty tree, refusing to compromise but now felled, in prison and about to lose his life?

In another piece of brilliant rabbinic teaching Jesus both praises John and explains him to the crowds. Comparing him to Elijah adds to the picture, but even Elijah eventually served the purpose God had for him and had to move aside for someone else (in his case, Elisha).

How wise are you?
(Matt. 11:16-19)

Jesus hasn't quite finished at this point. The crowds have criticised John for his asceticism, and Jesus for not being ascetic! So, in turn, Jesus criticises them for being fickle and flighty, as children can often be. What did they really want?

Jesus ends with another one of those puzzling statements that needs some explanation. In Matthew 11:19 we read, 'But wisdom is proved right by her actions', while the equivalent in Luke 7:35 maintains the analogy with children by saying, 'But wisdom is proved right by all her children.'

Interestingly, the slight difference in wording between the two gospels is not reflected in the Greek, which is identical in each case except for the extra 'all' (*panton*) in Luke. The Greek word *teknon* is simply translated in two distinct ways, 'actions' and 'children'. This seems to be because 'children' are offspring, and 'actions' can also be the offspring or outcomes of something, in this case, wisdom. So the literal rendering of 'and is justified the wisdom from all her children' is really an idiom for 'wisdom can be seen by what it produces'.

There is another Hebraic peculiarity which adds to our understanding of this phrase. In Hebrew, words often have more than one meaning but in some cases these meanings can be total opposites, the context being the determining factor in how the word should be understood. For instance, the same word can mean both 'come' and 'go'.

Here, 'wisdom' can mean either smartness or stupidity. Exactly which is usually decided by context. So this idiom is stating that one can tell whether wisdom is real wisdom or simply stupidity by the consistency or inconsistency of its argument, and the effect of the resulting action. The proverbial way of saying this is obviously more succinct and so this is how Jesus chose to criticise the crowds regarding their views on John and himself. The inconsistency of their arguments is a clear indication of their lack of wisdom.

The nearness of summer?

(Matt. 24:32-33)

Returning to things that are 'near', we find a further example in Matthew 24:32-33. In particular, the lesson of the fig tree, which, with its tender twigs and emerging leaves, tells us that summer is near. This occurs in a passage about the end times, so we might expect complexities and controversies. However, our aim here is to find connections of a Hebraic nature rather than solve conundrums.

252

The big debate usually surrounds the fig tree. Does it represent Israel? In the Bible, sometimes it does, but not always. A fig tree can be symbolic of something else, for instance in Proverbs 27:18, where it denotes a master.

'The one who guards a fig-tree will eat its fruit, and whoever protects their master will be honoured.'

The parallelism equates the fruit gained from tending your fig tree with the honour you receive from serving your master well.

Moreover, at times a fig tree is simply a fig tree, which may be all that is intended in Matthew 24:32. The lesson to be drawn is an uncomplicated one: you can tell by looking at a fig tree when summer is on the way. And it is with the word 'summer' that the main point is made, with a link (*remez!*) back to the prophet Amos.

In Amos 8:1-2, the prophet is asked by the Lord to describe the vision that he is being shown. He replies, literally, that he sees 'a basket of summer'. This is usually translated as 'summer fruits' or 'ripe fruit', which is a way of finishing what would otherwise seem to be an incomplete and peculiar sentence.

The Lord replies to Amos that the meaning of his vision is that the time is ripe for Israel, signifying that they are 'ripe' for judgement. The actual Hebrew has 'the end has come upon my people Israel', which fits well as 'summer' and 'end' are linked within the root system for Hebrew words (*qaitz* and *ha-qetz*, respectively), the logic being that summer is the end of the growing season and the agricultural year.

Of course, 'ripe' also depicts a similar idea. The fruit has reached full growth. All that remains is for a harvest to take place. In addition, the concept of a harvest illustrates judgement, in particular the separation of the good from the bad, as we have seen in some of Jesus' parables.

To summarise, Amos sees 'summer' (fruits) in a basket, which speaks of an 'end' which, in turn, relates to judgement. Likewise, in his lesson of the fig tree, Jesus made the same connection between summer and judgement. He wanted to reinforce what he had just been telling his disciples about the end times and final judgement. Effectively, Jesus is saying, you can read the signs that a fig tree gives out, so when you see happening all these things I've been describing, then know that I am near.

How near is near?

Right at the door. As close at that. No distance at all.

We have one final chapter in which we will complete our survey of gospel texts whose meaning often puzzles or eludes us. In particular, we will attempt to discover how God's memory works.

Chapter Twenty-Five

Remember Me

Luke 6:22, 9:29, 51, 23:42

As stated at the beginning of the previous chapter, we will now be largely in Luke. And as hinted at the end of it, we will be explaining what it means for God to remember (and forget) someone (or something). But before then, three more snippets from Luke.

Reject your name as evil
(Luke 6:22)

In Luke chapter 6 we find Jesus delivering his 'sermon on the plain', a shorter but otherwise equivalent version of the 'sermon on the mount' which Matthew records. Some of the Beatitudes are included (Luke 6:20-22) and it is in one of these that we come across another one of those puzzling phrases which requires some attention.

'Blessed are you when people . . . reject your name as evil' (Luke 6:22). What exactly does this mean? The Authorised Version has 'cast out your name as evil', which might help a little but still hasn't made it totally clear. For that we need, as usual, to listen to the Jewish Jesus.

In Hebrew, adjectives come after the noun, so what we effectively have is 'name evil' or 'name bad'. Moreover, the word 'as' doesn't occur in this sentence but was added in both the Greek and the English as 'cast out your name bad' doesn't make so much sense.

In Luke 6:22 the Greek verb is *ekbalosin*, which comes from *ekballo*. This does mean to cast out or throw out, but usually in a forceful way, whereas the Hebrew equivalent, *hotzi*, contains no sense of anything vigorous or violent. Rather, it is a causative form of 'go out', so it should be understood as 'to cause to go out or come out'.

In general terms this means to make something public. Today we might express this as 'publish' or 'issue', and, in particular, if what is being publicised is a bad name then we call it defamation or slander.

We see this phrase in the Old Testament when Nehemiah realised that men had been hired to intimidate him so he would commit a sin and then 'they would give me a bad name to discredit me' (Neh. 6:13). More examples occur in Deuteronomy. For instance, 'If a man takes a wife and, after sleeping with her, dislikes her and slanders her and gives her a bad name . . .' (Deut. 22:13-14). Later in the same chapter we have '. . . because this mans has given an Israelite virgin a bad name' (Deut. 22:19).

With this understanding of the phrase 'reject your name as evil' we now know how to read Luke 6:22. We are to consider ourselves blessed when men smear our name or slander us on account of Jesus.

The face of Jesus
(Luke 9:29, 51)

Our next two examples come from Luke chapter 9, both involving the face of Jesus.

In the first of these, as part of the account of the transfiguration of Jesus, we read that 'the appearance of his face changed' (Luke 9:29), which is a very Hebraic phrase. This may not appear in the Old Testament but is found in rabbinic literature contemporary with Jesus. But what exactly was happening?

The Authorised Version has the rather expressive 'the fashion of his countenance was altered'. This somewhat old-fashioned language also attempts to follow the Greek, but still doesn't explain what kind of change took place. Nor does the word 'transfiguration' help as it is not that specific, simply meaning 'change' or 'alteration'. Nor does it appear in any of the gospel texts for this event, only in the general heading for the passage, so no further clue can be found there.

We do, however, learn something about the change in Jesus' face by turning to Matthew's version, which for once is less Hebraic in its description. There we find the simple evocation that 'his face shone like the sun' (Matt. 17:2).

If we want further illumination of our own, we can compare this with a similar transfiguration in the Old Testament, where Moses' face was radiant when he came down from Sinai with the tablets of the Law in his hands (Exod. 34:29) and whenever he entered the Lord's presence to speak with him (Exod. 34:34-35). It is therefore perhaps fitting that Moses was one of those present at the transfiguration to see what happened to Jesus, and even more so given what Luke tells us they spoke about. In the midst of the glorious splendour of the occasion they talked of Jesus' forthcoming death, described as his 'exodus' or 'departure' or *exodon* (Luke 9:31).

The other idiomatic use of 'face' in this chapter is in Luke 9:51, though it is not immediately apparent. The English text simply says that Jesus 'resolutely set out for Jerusalem'. However, the Greek does say he 'intently set his face to go to Jerusalem', which would match the similar Hebrew phrase behind this statement.

Hebrew loves anatomical idioms, many of which are about the face. Among others, you can flee from the face of, set your face against, turn your face from, make your face shine on, hide your face and lift up your face. The face is used to represent the person himself, which explains why there are also several places where God's Presence is literally his face, as in Exodus 33:14, 'My Presence will go with you.' How evocative it is to think of this as God's face walking with us!

The Hebraic idiom to 'set your face towards' or 'set your face to go somewhere' simply means to turn in the direction of that place and then set off. The phrase is found many times in the Old Testament. Examples include Genesis 31:21, 2 Kings 12:17 and Daniel 11:17. In each of these cases the Hebrew tells us that a face has been 'set', which is simply a way of indicating towards which place someone was intending to go or where he was *heading*. Notice that in English we prefer 'head' rather than 'face' when talking in these terms.

Problems begin to arise when a translator is keen to add something extra to make a particular point, such as in Daniel 11:17 where we read 'He will determine to come'. There is no specific determination in the Hebrew words used, though, of course, to determine to do something may simply be about making a decision rather than having anything more explicit in mind.

Similarly, in Luke 9:51, translators often overplay what the Greek (and Hebrew) is saying. For instance, the word 'intently' can simply express an intention. Translators and commentators often interpret this as something much greater with the use of 'resolutely' or expressions such as 'an iron will' or 'a face set like flint'. It should be noted that the phrase in Isaiah 50:7, 'I have set my face like flint', is in an entirely different context and for once no *remez* is involved.

So regarding Jesus, we should not assume or imply that anything showed on his face as he set off to Jerusalem. No gritted teeth. No putting on a brave face. No inner struggle as he decided to do something he didn't want to. The Hebrew idiom simply means 'as the time approached, he set off'. Clearly he was not going to turn back. It was the right time so there was intent on his part, but there is no sign he had to find extra courage or determination at this point.

It is worth noting that in Luke 9:53 the Greek is literally 'he was travelling with his face set towards Jerusalem' but here it is now better translated as 'he was heading for Jerusalem'. We might say he was following his nose!

Remember me

(Luke 23:42)

Now let's turn our attention away from faces and consider God's memory, as promised earlier (if I recall correctly!).

Several times in Scripture we read that God remembered someone; for instance, Noah (Gen. 8:1), Rachel (Gen. 30:22), Hannah (1 Sam. 1:19). In what way does this make sense? Does God occasionally have a memory lapse, a senior moment, and then suddenly recall who these people are? During the one hundred and fifty days of the waters flooding the earth had Noah slipped God's mind?

And what should we make of that tremendous statement that God remembers our sins no more (Isa. 43:25, Jer. 31:34)? We would hope this is not just a temporary brain fade!

The answer is that in Hebraic terms, 'remember' is nothing to do with the memory and everything to do with the will. Biblically, to remember means to do someone a favour or intervene on their behalf. It involves making a choice and acting for someone's benefit.

On a purely human level, consider what happened to Joseph while in prison. His two fellow inmates, Pharaoh's chief cupbearer and chief baker, both had a dream one night. Joseph delivered a favourable interpretation to the chief cupbearer, assuring him that in three days he would be out of prison and back in his old job. In return, Joseph asked for a favour: 'When all goes well with you, remember me and show me kindness' (Gen. 40:14). Basically, put in a good word to Pharaoh on my behalf and get me out of here!

Of course, the message of the dream came true. However, the chief cupbearer 'did not remember Joseph; he forgot him' (Gen. 40:23). It is hardly likely the chief cupbearer couldn't remember this strange guy he had 'done time with' in prison, or that he had forgotten the dream and its interpretation. Rather, what the text is telling us is that he chose not to do what Joseph had asked him.

But God isn't like that. He doesn't 'remember' or 'forget' as a man does. For him to remember (or, in the case of our sins, not remember) refers to an obligation. 'Remember' Is a word which invokes God's promises and commitments, especially with regard to his covenants with men. When God 'remembered Noah' (Gen. 8:1) it meant it was now time to act on his behalf and cause the water to recede from the earth. With Rachel and Hannah, it was time in God's purposes to 'open their wombs' and enable them to conceive (Gen. 30:22, 1 Sam. 1:19).

After Noah had emerged from the ark, God made a covenant with him and every living creature. God promised to remember that covenant for all time (Gen. 9:15, 16), and set a rainbow in the clouds as a visual sign, not so much as a memory jogger for himself but so mankind might remember there was a permanent covenant in place.

Another covenant-based example is mentioned in Exodus 2:24. When the Israelites were in slavery in Egypt, 'God heard their groaning and he remembered his covenant with Abraham, with Isaac and with Jacob.' As a result he decided to act and set them free.

Another instance occurs in Leviticus 26:42 where God states, 'I will remember my covenant with Jacob and my covenant with Isaac and my covenant with Abraham, and I will remember the land.' Further examples can be found in Leviticus 26:45 and 1 Chronicles 16:15.

God's covenant promises require him to take action on behalf of his people. This was known as 'remembering the covenant'. The same was also intended to apply in reverse to Israel. When Israel was told to remember the commandments it meant more than just recall they have something written down somewhere. They must choose to do them! This is why they were told to make tassels and put them on the corners of their garments. 'You will have these tassels to look at and so you will remember all the commands of the Lord, that you may obey them and not prostitute yourselves by going after the lusts of your own hearts and eyes' (Num. 15:39-40). As visual reminders of their covenant with God, the tassels were a spur to obedience and action.

The psalmist often displayed this same idea when he pleaded for God to remember him and hence help him. For instance, 'Remember me, O Lord, when you show favour to your people, come to my aid when you save them' (Ps. 106:4).

As we round off this theme, let's bring it closer to home. We should now realise that when God promises to 'remember our sins no more' he is saying that because of his covenant with us through Christ, he will take no further action against us. What a glorious thought!

As a final encouragement, one more remembrance text. A dying thief on the cross next to Jesus had enough insight and breath left to make an appeal to another dying man,

'Jesus, remember me when you come into your kingdom' (Luke 23:42). How remarkable that he saw a king hanging there. And how wonderful that he used a covenant word of salvation – remember me! It is not surprising that Jesus' reply was so reassuring: 'Today you will be with me in paradise' (Luke 23:43).

'Remember' is a word we can use for ourselves when talking to God in any circumstance, however desperate, whatever our need. Short and to the point. Remember me! God will surely respond.

One final observation. Did you notice how Jesus began his reply to the dying thief? 'I tell you the truth.' Amen!!

And Finally . . .

Amen, indeed! The dying thief had it absolutely right! He had recognised the man on the cross next to him as someone who had a kingdom, and he wanted to be part of it. Remember me! Jesus' response was typically Hebraic when he used a phrase we looked at in a previous chapter: 'I tell you the truth'. 'Yes!' Jesus is saying, 'You've got it right! I am a king, and I will indeed remember you. In fact, I'll see you in paradise later today.'

Under different circumstances this man may have become a disciple of Jesus. He may have longed to listen more to the Jewish Jesus. Unfortunately, he had no time left for this. At least in his final hours he had made the one decision that mattered, and so was invited into the kingdom of God. But for him, discipleship was not possible.

For most of us, however, we do not come to Christ that late in life, so we have no valid reason not to devote the rest of our lives to being a true follower of Jesus. But do we choose to do so?

We need to realise that being a believer is not the same as being a disciple. Coming to faith is only the start of the journey, and the process of turning a believer into a disciple is not automatic or easy. There is much that can prevent this happening.

We have seen that a disciple allows someone else to shape their life. From birth, we are all influenced by others. We learn how to live our lives from those immediately around us, or those we read or hear about. This happens naturally and continually through life. You are definitely a disciple of somebody, maybe many people. But if you are a Christian, are you *his* disciple? Is Christ your teacher and guide through life? Are you yoked to Jesus in the way that he offers?

To be a disciple of Jesus is to be with him daily, learning with others how to live in the kingdom of God. A disciple has a strong desire to be like his rabbi and to do what he does. For a believer in Christ, this should become the obvious way to live. It should also be clear for others to see. 'There goes a disciple of Jesus ...'

Christians often talk of becoming more like Jesus, being transformed into his likeness. But is this our actual experience? Being just a casual follower or even a churchgoer doesn't make this happen. Going to church does not make you a disciple. In fact, you can be a disciple without actually joining a church, though you cannot be a disciple on your own. You need others equally determined to follow this path. This is the meaning and purpose behind the word *ekklesia*, which we mentioned in Chapter Seven.

An *ekklesia* is a community of believers with Jesus as their Head. This is what Jesus promised to build, not an institutional organisation or hierarchical structure full of programmes and activities or even religious services. Just because something is called a church or has 'church' as part of its name, doesn't mean it is an *ekklesia* in the New Testament sense. An *ekklesia* is a spiritual home for disciples, a place where discipleship can flourish.

Once we have decided to commit ourselves to living 'the Jesus way' we need to listen carefully to what he said. During our studies we have seen that Jesus' teaching methods were very different from those we usually expect today. In particular, *what* Jesus said often cannot be properly understood without knowing *how* he said it or without taking into account the world and culture in which he was teaching.

Jesus' aim was not primarily to impart knowledge or information, but to impact people's lives so that they are transformed. This may involve information transfer, but disciples are never meant to be just listeners, empty receptacles waiting to be filled. Today, we usually test if someone has learnt something by seeing if they can repeat it by reproducing it in language rather than in actions. That is not how Jesus operated. He wanted to see his teaching being lived out.

What you have read in these pages is not really new, though much of it may have been so for you. Rather, this has been about recovering what has been lost or ignored for centuries. In the past many churches embraced a way of thinking that goes under the name of Replacement Theology. In this, it is claimed that God has rejected the Jews and replaced them with a new people, sometimes referred to incorrectly as a new 'Israel'. In short, God changed his mind, broke his covenant promises to Abraham, Isaac and Jacob, and decided to start again. Whether he did this out of anger or frustration or dissatisfaction, it doesn't reflect well on God! Which is one good reason why it is false.

One major consequence of such a view is that it hides the essential Jewishness of Jesus and replaces him with a Jesus of our own making. It also denies the Jewish nature of the early *ekklesia*, and the fact that for some time the vast majority of disciples were Jewish. This book is offered as a contribution towards returning us to how things were by rediscovering the ancient paths. Re-replacing, if you like.

Let's return to the scriptures for two final points.

Firstly, the gospels record several occasions when Jesus began a sentence with 'I am ...' We have already looked at one of these in Chapter Twenty-Three: 'I am the true vine' (John 15:1). Six others are also found in John's Gospel, as is one of the most intriguing statements Jesus ever made: 'Before Abraham was born, I am!' (John 8:58). Jesus was nearly stoned to death for saying this. Why did this provoke such an extreme reaction? Perhaps the answer lies in the Old Testament. Maybe Jesus was hinting at something!

In fact, it was more than a hint. It was a resounding, unmissable echo of the time when Moses met God at the bush which was on fire but did not burn up. There Moses was told about his mission, to go to Pharaoh and bring the Israelites out of Egypt. Naturally he was a bit tentative, even scared. Why would the Israelites believe him? Who should he say had sent him? So Moses asked God to reveal his name. The answer came back, 'I AM WHO I AM. This is what you are to say to the Israelites: "I AM has sent me to you"' (Exod. 3:14).

Jesus is therefore making huge claims about himself with this 'I am' statement. Not just that he somehow pre-existed Abraham. That would be extraordinary enough. But here is a declaration of deity, of an identity that makes him equal to God himself.

In all our study of Jesus as a Jewish rabbi we should never forget how much more than that he really was, and still is. He is the Son of God, at one with the Father who sent him. He came into a particular culture at a particular time and ministered in a particular way, but he is also the eternal Word of God. He existed with God from the beginning and yet became flesh in order to live as a human being among other human beings.

Secondly, there was one occasion when Jesus deliberately *didn't* open his mouth and speak. At one point during his trial, which was in many ways a complete mockery, full of injustice and illegality, he was brought before Herod. That's Herod Antipas, whom you will recall from Chapter Twenty-One was in charge in Galilee and whom Jesus referred to as 'that fox' (Luke 13:32). But Jesus is on trial in Jerusalem, out of Herod's territory, so how does Jesus get brought before him? And why does Jesus remain silent?

Jesus didn't so much have one trial but several. It all started with the Jewish Council, then Jesus went before Pilate. After that he was sent to Herod and finally back to Pilate who condemned him to death.

When Pilate was told that Jesus was a Galilean he realised this put him under Herod's jurisdiction. As Herod was in Jerusalem for Passover, Pilate thought he could shift the responsibility of this awkward case onto Herod. Nice try, but it didn't work! (See Luke 23:5-7.)

Luke continues: 'When Herod saw Jesus, he was greatly pleased, because for a long time he had been wanting to see him. From what he had heard about him, he hoped to see him perform a sign of some sort. He plied him with many questions, but Jesus *gave him no answer'* (Luke 23:8-9, italics mine).

Many times when Jesus was in Galilee, Herod could have gone to see him, but he didn't. He sent death threats instead. Now Jesus has nothing to say to him. Herod's questions, whatever they were, remained unanswered.

In one of the most telling prophetic passages about the Messiah, we read: 'He was oppressed and afflicted, yet he did not open his mouth; he was led like a lamb to the slaughter, and as a sheep before its shearers is silent, so he did not open his mouth' (Isa. 53:7).

Even though innocent, Jesus didn't object to being put to death. He fulfilled the role of the suffering servant for our sake. Once more, in all our study of Jesus as a Jewish rabbi we should never forget how much more than that he really was, and still is. He is our Saviour, the one who can redeem us from our sin and bring us back to God.

We end our studies at this point, but no contemplation of Jesus is ever complete. There is always more to discover. Like many of the parables he taught, the story of Jesus is left unfinished, waiting for us to place ourselves into that story, to make it ours and bring it to a personal conclusion.

Jesus is rabbi, Saviour, Lord. Is that what he means to you?

Appendix A

Parables in the Old Testament

Judges 9:8-15	Parable of the Trees (a portent of judgement)
2 Samuel 12:1-4	Parable of the Ewe Lamb (a juridical parable)
2 Samuel 14:4-7	Parable of the Two Brothers
1 Kings 20:38-43	Parable of the Escaped Prisoner
2 Kings 14:8-10	The Thistle and the Cedar (a fable)
Isaiah 5:1-7	Song of the Vineyard (a juridical parable)
Ezekiel 17:2-10	Parable of the Eagles and the Vine (a riddle)
Ezekiel 19:1-9	Parable of the Lioness
Ezekiel 19:10-14	Parable of the Vine (allusion to Isaiah chapter 5)
Ezekiel 20:45-49	Parable of the Forest Fire
Ezekiel 24:2-5	Parable of the Seething Pot (an object lesson)

Telling the Truth

In Chapter Twenty-Two we looked at the phrase 'I tell you the truth' which Jesus used repeatedly. Here is the full list.

Matthew	Mark	Luke	John
5:18, 26	3:28	4:2	1:51
6:2, 5, 16	8:12	12:37	3:3, 5, 11
8:10	9:1, 41	18:17, 29	5:19, 24, 25
10:15, 23, 42	10:15, 29	21:32	6:26, 32, 47, 53
11:11	11:23	23:43	8:34, 51, 58
13:17	12:43		10:1, 7
16:28	13:30		12:24
17:20	14:9, 18, 25, 30		13:16, 20, 21, 38
18:3, 13, 18			14:12
19:23, 28			16:20, 23
21:21, 31			21:18
23:36			
24:2, 34, 47			
25:12, 40, 45			
26:13, 21, 34			

Notes:

In some cases 'you' is singular, for instance when Jesus is addressing Peter rather than the crowds (Matt. 26:34).

In two additional cases to those listed above (Luke 12:44, 21:3), the Greek is slightly different (*aleithos lego umin*) and so the translation would more accurately be 'of a truth I say to you'.

In every reference in John, the truth is 'doubled', as in 'truly, truly'.

Suggested Further Reading

Andy Angel, *The Jesus You* Really *Didn't Know* (Cascade)

Kenneth Bailey, *Jesus through Middle Eastern Eyes* (SPCK)

David Biven, *New Light on the Difficult Words of Jesus* (En-Gedi Resource Center)

Robby Gallaty, *The Forgotten Jesus* (Zondervan)

Joseph Gisbey, *Follow* (Darton, Longman and Todd)

Lois Tverberg, *Walking in the Dust of Rabbi Jesus* (Zondervan)

Lois Tverberg and Ann Spangler, *Sitting at the Feet of Rabbi Jesus* (Zondervan)

Brad Young, *The Newer Testament* (Hebrew Heritage Bible Society)

Brad Young, *Jesus the Jewish Theologian* (Hendrickson)

Brad Young, *Meet the Rabbis* (Hendrickson)

Index of Scripture and Ancient Sources

Not including scriptures in appendices

EXTRA-BIBLICAL SOURCES

Also by Paul Luckraft

The Wall and the Word

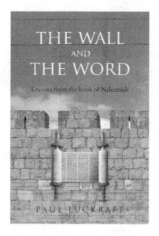

ISBN: 978-1-915046-54-3

Nehemiah is best known for its account of the rebuilding of the wall of Jerusalem by the Israelites on returning from exile. But there is much more to the book than this. Equally important was the need to rebuild the people as God's community. How could they be reformed to live according to his will? For this they needed to rediscover what God had said in the Book of the Law.

Paul Luckraft examines each chapter to draw out the main lessons. Why did Nehemiah face a lot of opposition from many enemies, and what can we learn from his experiences? What exactly was this 'Book of the Law' and is this relevant to us now? Why was rediscovering the Feast of Tabernacles so important for them, and what can this mean for us?

Nehemiah is a largely forgotten book, but an essential part of our 'God-breathed' scripture. It's time to let it breathe again as we seek to rebuild ourselves as a community of believers and strengthen our own lives in his service.